Sylvan Musings, or, The Spirit of the Woods

LONDON.
SPOTTISWOODES and SHAW,
New-street-Square.

SYLVAN MUSINGS;

OR,

THE SPIRIT OF THE WOODS.

BY MRS. HEY.

" Move along these shades
In *gentleness of heart* ; with gentle hand
Touch — for *there is a spirit in the woods.*"

" These trees shall be my books,
And in their barks my thoughts I'll character."

LONDON:

LONGMAN, BROWN, GREEN, AND LONGMANS,

PATERNOSTER-ROW.

1849.

PREFACE.

THE first step in any new career is confessedly the most difficult; that step, however, once taken, every succeeding one becomes comparatively easy: this is especially true with regard to authorship.

When the writer of the present work gave her volume on flowers to the public, she contemplated with full as much fear as hope the novel position in which she had placed herself, and almost started

"E'en at the sounds herself had made."

Her apprehensions were, however, soon allayed by the favour, so much beyond her most sanguine anticipations, with which her publication was received. This reception, if it did not suggest, at least greatly encouraged her in her present undertaking, the subject of which leads her to hope that those who listened kindly to her lays on flowers, will not less favourably regard her sylvan musings.

The transition seemed natural and easy from the flower which decks the greensward to the tree that shelters it. The main difficulty was how to vary the reflections and imagery sufficiently in subjects so nearly allied; to effect which, as far as possible, the author has in many instances introduced the tree incidentally, instead of making it the sole burden of the poem.

Of all inanimate objects, trees are the most companionable. Every breath of air makes them vocal, and they "discourse most eloquent music," apparently adapting their tones to the mood of the listener. Is he sorrowful?—they seem to share his sadness; is he joyous?—to partake his mirth; is he religious?—his devotion. For him there is not only " pleasure," but society, " in the pathless woods ;" for he peoples them with " calling shapes,"

" And airy tongues that syllable men's names."

How beautiful is a wooded landscape! Be the season what it may, trees always excite admir-

ation. The tender green of spring, the deeper
tints and full-grown foliage of summer, the surpassing glory and variety of autumn, and even
the snow and hoarfrost of winter, each sits so
well upon them, that, delighted with the present
impression, we think no other vesture would
become them so well.

The individuality of character, too, which each
tree possesses, adds an indescribable charm to
sylvan scenery. " What can afford more delightful contrast in landscape," says a tasteful author, " than the giant strength of the oak with
the flexile elegance of the ash; the stately tranquillity of the elm with the tremulous lightness of
the poplar ; the bright and vivid foliage of the
beech or sycamore with the funeral majesty of
the cedar or the yew ; all differing in form and
character as in colour ?"

> " No tree in all the grove but has its charms,
> And each its charm peculiar."

If the reader partake the enthusiasm of the
writer towards the whole leafy race, he will at
least approve her subject : for the manner in

which she has handled it she craves his indulgence. To herself, at all events, the task has been a most pleasant one, for during its progress she has wandered "fancy free"

> " By the rushy-fringed bank
> Where grows the willow and the osier dank; "

and, anon,

> " To arched walks of twilight groves,
> And shadows brown, that sylvan loves,
> Of pine, or monumental oak,
> Where the rude axe, with heaved stroke,
> Was never heard the nymphs to daunt,
> Or fright them from their hallow'd haunt. "

A source of great additional interest has been the preparation of the drawings for the illustration of the work, which the author herself has ventured to execute from nature, and which she trusts will be found botanically correct.

With regard to the arrangement of the different subjects, in compliment to the British sylva, the volume is opened with some of the most celebrated trees which compose it; but subsequently no particular plan has been followed, the pieces having been placed indiscriminately as fancy dictated.

CONTENTS.

LIST OF PLATES.

INTRODUCTION.

WHERE is the snow-wreath that but yesterday
Crested yon mountain's brow? the icy chain
Which held the waters in subjection, where?
A breath from " the sweet south" hath melted them;
And, hark! how yon freed brook, as it pursues
Its seaward track, proclaims rejoicingly
To hill and valley, that sweet Spring has come!

Yes, Spring *has* come, with light and beauty crown'd;
And where her dews have fall'n on mead or bower,
Or the light pressure of her foot hath been,
Up starts at once a galaxy of flowers,
Each in its tiny chalice offering up
Whate'er it hath of fragrance, at her shrine;
Nor lacks there fitting music, for the breeze
Steals from each bush a song, and with it blends
Its own soft cadences, so wildly sweet.
Nature keeps holyday, and man himself
Partakes her triumph and imbibes her joy;
Sickness revives, and Grief forgets to weep;
And many a harp which on the willows hung

Is tuned afresh to notes of joy and praise.
Mine, too, is strung, albeit unskilfully,
And on its chords my trembling hand is laid:
Yet is it mute, because unfix'd my theme;
For, whilst my eye " the landscape measures round,"
Hill, valley, stream, each woos my roving glance,
And asks the tribute of admiring song.
Once more I gaze,—ah! how could I o'erlook
Yon low-roof'd cottage with its shadowing tree?
How pass unmark'd that grove, whose varied hues
Do more than rival Autumn's tints of gold?
Or, in the distance, waking thoughts sublime,
Yon forest stretching to th' horizon's verge?
No more I hesitate,—wake, harp of mine,
To *sylvan beauty* give thy votive lay.

" Hail, ye patrician trees !" th' ambitious muse,
Who, late, in lowlier mood, did wreath her lyre
With the wild flowers that at your foot diffuse
Their never-cloying sweets, doth now aspire
To do *ye* homage: — not that she doth tire
Of mead or hedgerow with their varied bloom;
But there are moments when she would retire
From laughing landscape, to your cloister'd gloom,
For higher, holier flights her wearied wing to plume.

" Hail, ye patrician trees ! " I love ye well,
Whate'er your aspect and whate'er your mood;
Alike when Spring with her resistless spell
First on your boughs unfolds the tender bud,
As when by Summer's shower and sunshine woo'd
In " leafy luxury" ye stand array'd;
Nor less when mournful Autumn has imbued
With her own sadness bower and forest glade,
Or when 'neath Winter's blight your latest glories fade.

I love ye when in congregated pride
The forest's shadowy vastness ye assume,
And when in softer beauty, side by side,
To hill and vale ye lend your grateful gloom.
I love ye when with consecrated bloom
The village church ye reverently embower;
Nor scarcely less when by the peasant's home,
Or on the green, in single pomp ye tower,
As if ye loved to grace the dwellings of the poor.

Nor owns the eye alone your potent spell,
The soul of music lingers 'mid your boughs;
Like harp e'er tuned, 'tis yours to sink or swell
Responsive to each varying blast which blows.

Let but the storm your slumbering might arouse, ·
Then, sylvan minstrels, is your power confess'd;
Anon, when Eve, with breath "that shuts the rose"
Just stirs your leaves with motion that seems rest,
Oh! with what low sweet notes ye soothe the aching breast!

For this I love ye—yea, that ye appear
Instinct with human feeling! not a tone
Which the lips utter, mirthful or severe,
But ye can make the thrilling sounds your own;
Devotion's choral chant,—grief's dirge-like moan,—
Triumph's loud swell,—affection's gentle sigh,
And those low murmurs breathing peace alone,
Soft as a mother's evening lullaby,
When she would seal in sleep her infant's drooping eye.

One other strain ye have, a warning strain,
Its burden this, "Man as a leaf doth fade!"
Oh! happy he who hears it not in vain,
He to whose chasten'd fancy woodland glade,
And far-spread forest with its depth of shade,
Become a temple; to whom flower and tree
The ministers of holy truths are made,
Reminding him, though passing frail he be,
His glorious, awful dower is immortality.

THE

SPIRIT OF THE WOODS.

THE OAK.

QUERCUS ROBUR.

" Happy Britannia !
Rich is thy soil, and merciful thy clime ;
Unmatch'd thy guardian oaks."

THE oak is the glory of the British sylva. What the
palm is to the tribes of the desert, and the banian to
the inhabitants of the East, such is the oak to Britons.
It is our citadel, the basis of our strength; and whilst
we possess it,

" Britannia needs no bulwark,
No towers along her steep ;
Her march is o'er the mountain waves,
Her home is on the deep.

B

With thunders from her native oak,
She quells the floods below —
As they roar on the shore,
When the stormy tempests blow;
When the battle rages loud and long,
And the stormy tempests blow."

How suitable is its appearance to its destination! It looks as if made to contend with, and surmount, difficulties. Its deep, searching roots, its broad base, stout sinewy limbs, and knotted branches, all bespeak it fitted to war with the elements; whilst the quality of its timber, that of elasticity, toughness, and strength, points out its admirable adaptation to the wants of a naval country. "Many kinds of wood," says Gilpin, "are *harder*, as box and ebony; many kinds are *tougher*, as yew and ash; but it is supposed no species of wood—at least no species of timber—is possessed of both these qualities together in so great a degree as British oak." But strength is not the only characteristic in the appearance of the oak: it combines beauty with strength, and the result is, a lordly dignity of aspect, which entitles it to be

" Sole king of forests all."

Virgil describes the oak, not only with the glow of a

poet, but with the precision of a naturalist; every peculiarity is noticed, and with such effect, that his description has the vividness and reality of a painting. Our own poets, in unnumbered passages, many of them of great beauty, have done homage to this tree; but to select from so ample a store would be a work of time and labour; to quote all, a thing impossible.

The oak is remarkable for its slowness of growth, and amazing longevity. It lives to a patriarchal age, well deserving the emphatic epithet of "monumental oak," bestowed on it by Milton.

There may be something fanciful in Shenstone's comparison between this noble tree and our national character; but as it is complimentary, and, on the whole, tolerably correct, it shall have a place here. "Oaks," says he, "are in all respects the image of the manly character: in former times, I should have said, and in present times I think I am authorised to say, the British one. As a brave man is not suddenly either elated by prosperity, or depressed by adversity, so the oak displays not its verdure on the sun's first approach, nor drops it on his first departure: add to this its majestic appearance, the rough grandeur of its bark, and the wide protection of its branches. A large spreading, aged oak is, perhaps, the most venerable of all inanimate objects."

Independently of its more valuable qualities, the true "unwedgable and gnarled oak" of Shakspeare is the most picturesque of all the trees which adorn real English scenery. "It refuses no subject either in natural or artificial landscape. It is suited to the grandest, and may be introduced into the most pastoral, and even rustic, scene : ——

> ' Hard by, a cottage chimney smokes
> From betwixt two aged oaks.'

It adds dignity to the ruined tower and Gothic arch, and throws its arms with propriety over the purling brook, or the mantling pool."

To crown its other excellencies, as has been already observed, no tree can bear up so well against the tempest ; indeed, it is supposed to acquire greater stability of root from every contest with the elements, and to thrive

> " E'en by the rude concussion of the storm."

> " Mark yonder oaks ! superior to the power
>   Of all the warring winds of heaven they rise,
>   And from the stormy promontory tower
>   And toss their giant arms amid the skies,
> While each assailing blast increase of strength supplies."

We are reminded by this noble characteristic of a
spirited passage in one of the best periodicals of the
day : —

" Those old oaks seem sullen in the sunshine, and slow to put forth
their power, like the spirit of the land they emblem.   But they, too, are
relaxing from their wonted sternness : soon will that faint green be a
glorious yellow ; and while the gold-laden boughs stoop boldly to the
storms with which they love to dally, bounds not the heart of every
Briton to the music of the national anthem —

> ' Rule Britannia !
> Britannia rule the waves !' ? "

Proud monarch of the forest !
    That once, a sapling bough,
Didst quail far more at evening's breath
    Than at the tempest now,
Strange scenes have pass'd, long ages roll'd
    Since first upon thy stem,
Then weak as osier twig, Spring set
    Her leafy diadem.

Perchance thy mid-day glory
    Long since has pass'd away, ˙
Yet who that views thy giant bulk
    Can link thee with decay?
No blight is on thy leaves, no branch
    From thy huge trunk is torn,
And still in conscious might thou laugh'st
    The hurricane to scorn.

And many a summer's bravery
    Each ample bough shall grace,
And many an angry winter's storm
    Thy hoary vigour brace,
Unless at call of " hearts of oak "
    Beneath the axe thou bow,
To bear the brunt of battle's rage
    And thunder on the foe.

To thee but little recks it
    What seasons come or go,
Thou lovest to breathe the gale of spring
    And bask in summer's glow,
But more to feel the wintry winds
    Sweep by in awful mirth,
For well thou know'st each blast will fix
    Thy roots more deep in earth.

Would that to me life's changes
  Did thus with blessings come !
That mercies might, like gale of spring,
  Cause some new grace to bloom !
And that the storm which scattereth
  Each earth-born hope abroad,
Might anchor those of holier birth
  More firmly on my God !

THE ELM.

ULMUS CAMPESTRIS.

" Follow me, as I sing
And touch the warbled string ;
Under the shady roof
Of branching elm, star-proof,
Follow me ! "

THE elm is a very majestic tree; in beauty and dignity
yielding only to the oak.   Gilpin gives preference to the
ash in his scale of precedence, because it has more of
individuality than the elm, which he esteems a great
source of picturesque beauty; but he allows, at the same
time, that this want of distinctive character is observable
chiefly in its skeleton state: when in full leaf, the elm
shows itself an elm, and is marked by its superiority of
height to most other of our forest trees, and by the great
luxuriance of its shadowy foliage, which, however, never
looks heavy or ungraceful, owing to the smallness of the
leaves.

Some naturalists doubt its right to be considered a
native, and aver that we are indebted to the Romans

for its introduction amongst us; arguing, in support of this opinion, that it is not found in our aboriginal forests, and that it does not propagate its species by seeds, as is the case with indigenous trees, but by suckers: others, however, contend, that of the seven species which constitute this genus, two, namely, ulmus campestris, our common elm, and ulmus montana, the wych elm, or wych hazel, are certainly natives.

The latter, characterised by a much larger leaf, and less compactness of growth, flourishes both in England and Scotland, not only in the lowlands, but in the most northern parts of the island; indeed it is considered as true and characteristic an appendage of the wild, mountainous scenery of the sister-kingdom, as the birch, the rowan, or even the pine itself. As such, it has obtained the enviable distinction of being introduced in the beautiful opening stanzas to " the Lady of the Lake :"

> " Harp of the north ! that mouldering long hast hung
> On the witch elm that shades St. Fillan's spring."

The timber of the elm is hard-grained, and ranks high in point of utility: it is peculiarly fitted for works connected with water, as it bears, without injury, the extremes of drought and moisture. Its leaves, in seasons of scarcity, yield fodder for cattle, and were used and recommended for this purpose by the ancient Romans. " Of all the trees which grow in our woods," says Evelyn, " there is none which does better suffer transplantation than the elm; for you may remove a tree of twenty years' growth with undoubted success :" in proof of which he goes on to say, that " those incomparable walks and vistas of them, both at Aranjuez, Casal del Campo, Madrid, the Escurial, and other places of delight belonging to the King and grandees of Spain, are planted with such as they report Philip the Second caused to be brought out of England ; before which it does not appear there were any of those trees in Spain."

For purposes such as these, the " length of colonnade " and " shaded walks," the elm was formerly in great request. " Our fathers," who " knew the value of a screen," were wont to form of it those stately avenues which led to their hospitable mansions. Some few of these " monuments of ancient taste " are yet left to us ; but the spirit of modern improvement forbids such formal entrances to the newly erected edifice. How far, in thus discarding them, it acts either tastefully or wisely, let the poet decide, who thus beautifully and feelingly deplores the change : —

" Ye fallen avenues ! once more I mourn
   Your fate unmerited, once more rejoice
   That yet a remnant of your race survives.
   How airy and how light the graceful arch !
   Yet awful as the consecrated roof
   Re-echoing pious anthems ! while beneath
   The checker'd earth seems restless as a flood
   Brush'd by the wind.   So sportive is the light
   Shot through the boughs, it dances as they dance,
   Shadow and sunshine intermingling quick,
   And dark'ning and enlight'ning, as the leaves
   Play wanton, ev'ry moment, ev'ry spot."

Judging from the frequency of his allusions to it, the elm must have been held in high esteem by Cowper. Describing one of his rambles, he says, —

———— " There, fast rooted in their bank,
Stand, never overlook'd, our favourite elms."

Thus, again, in his sketch of " the *peasant's nest*," —

" 'Tis perch'd upon the green hill-top, but close
   Environ'd with a ring of branching elms,
   That overhang the thatch."

And once more, —

———— " The grove receives us next,
Between the upright shafts of whose tall elms
We may discern the thresher at his task."

" Though a tree of consort, sociable, and affecting to
grow in company," the elm is not a forester; it demands
more ample room for the due expansion both of its
roots and branches, than the forest generally affords:
hence it is better fitted for the park and the lawn;
yet it by no means confines itself to such aristocratic
situations; not less it loves " dingle and bushy dell,"
and homely hedgerow also, where, indeed, it is perhaps
more frequently met with than any other tree; thus
exemplifying the propriety of Milton's epithet of
" hedgerow elms."

The Romans used to train the vine round the elm,
which afforded their poets many fanciful allusions, —
allusions which have been followed out by our own
bards. Thus Milton says, —

——————— " they led the vine
To wed her elm."

And Beaumont, —

——————— " the amorous vine
Doth with the fair and straight-limb'd elm entwine."

While Shakspeare, more true to English scenery, sub-
stitutes the ivy for the vine: —

————— " the female ivy so
Enrings the barky fingers of the elm."

With us it is consecrated to more solemn scenes, being
generally associated with the yew in adorning our
churchyards : —

" Beneath those rugged elms, that yew-tree's shade,
   Where heaves the turf in many a mouldering heap,
Each in his narrow cell for ever laid,
   The rude forefathers of the hamlet sleep."

Whether we borrowed this custom, as some suppose,
from our heathen conquerors, who, regarding the elm
and cypress as fruitless and therefore funereal trees,
planted them by the graves of their deceased heroes, it is
difficult to determine.   It would be more pleasing to
conjecture, that our Christian ancestors, observing it to
be one of the first trees that vivified at the touch of
spring, chose it on that account to betoken the resurrection of the dead.

   Trees are full of moral associations; regarded under
which impression, they possess even " something than
beauty dearer."   Many of them are rich in historic interest, and chronicle events of national importance;
others confine themselves to a more limited range of observation, and, recalling the memory of some renowned

individual, lead us beneath their shade to "hold high converse with the mighty dead." But where this peculiar charm is wanting, imagination bodies forth scenes and stories of its own creating, and "gives to airy nothing a local habitation and a name." An aged tree points to the past, a sapling to the future; and whilst the mind is exercised in these remote contemplations, we feel the force of Dr. Johnson's well-known observation : —

"Whatever withdraws us from the power of our senses, — whatever makes the past, the distant, or the future predominate over the present, — advances us in the dignity of thinking beings."

The elm, however, is a tree which records events not only of individual or national, but of universal, interest. It was beneath an elm that Penn signed his celebrated treaty with the Indians. It was near an elm that the saintly Hooper suffered martyrdom ! For a most heart-stirring account of that event the reader is referred to Soames' interesting and learned History of the Reformation, a short abstract from which we here subjoin : —
"Having reached the spot where stood the preparations* for his painful end, he knelt down and spent

* "Which was near unto the great elm-tree over against the college of priests, where he was wont to preach." — FOXE.

about half an hour in prayer. Having prepared himself for immolation, he requested of the spectators to repeat the Lord's prayer with him, and to pray for him while he should continue in the agonies of death. Instantly arose the voice of prayer, interrupted by sobs and groans from every quarter of the crowded area. He then ascended to the stake, and irons were brought to fasten him to it. 'You need not,' said he, 'thus to trouble yourselves. I doubt not but God will vouchsafe me strength to abide the fire's extremity without bands.' A chain, however, for the waist, he willingly allowed to be drawn around him; admitting that the frailty of his flesh might make him swerve from his position. Bundles of reeds were now thrown on the pile, some of which the sufferer embraced in his arms; and he calmly gave directions for the placing of others. Flame being added to the mass of fuel, its progress was, to feeling spectators, most painfully slow. Much of the wood was green, and violent gusts of wind blew the devouring element away from the victim." But why minutely trace the several details of this most horrid tragedy? He bore his agonies, which were prolonged through more than three quarters of an hour, with admirable constancy, moving incessantly his lips in prayer.

Wake, mountain breeze! why thus in time of need
Fold'st thou in languid listlessness thy wings?
Now, when broad noon o'er hill, and dale, and mead,
With conscious might his beamy standard flings;
Ye murmuring streamlets, that were wont to make
Music, how meet for summer's burning hour!
Ah! why, perfidious, do ye now forsake
Your pebbly beds? — ye, who did tempt the flower,
With promise bland, to ope its golden eye
Upon your shelving marge, and leave it thus to die!

From you, ye false ones, to the sylvan realm
I turn my steps; and see! yon glorious elm
Proffers so close a shade, that e'en the dew
(As if cool morn still o'er the green-sward threw
Her sheltering veil) within the chalic'd flower
Lies safe, unconscious of the noontide hour.
Here, then, where scarce a straggling beam invades
The leafy twilight, — here, where eve's soft shades
Seem stealing on mid-day, embower'd I'll lie
Till Phœbus' steeds shall gain the western sky;
And thoughts, like lights and shadows o'er the grass,
As bright as transient, o'er my mind shall pass:
Sweet summer-moods, — a visionary throng,
To which fond Fancy's fairest dreams belong.

Come, then, sweet Fancy, playful power!
And share with me my sylvan bower;
Bring all thy magic to beguile
Life's dull realities awhile.
Now shift the scene to moonlit glade
Where " dapper elves," beneath the shade
Of oak or elm, their revels keep,
What time we plodding mortals sleep.
Next, lead me to some haunted grove,
Such as the Fauns and Dryads love;
Or seat me by some brook, whose swell
Makes music, like a Naiad's shell:
Then touch the tree 'neath which I lie,
Till it unclose to ear and eye
Whate'er it may have heard or seen
Since Spring first cloth'd its stems with green.

Doubtless, sweet childhood, ever gay,
Hath sported here through summer day;
Doubtless, beneath its shading boughs
Lovers have met to breathe their vows;
Manhood, his future path to scheme;
Age, o'er the bygone time to dream;
And, haply, when day's garish pride
Had pass'd away — at eventide —

c

Some lonely saint would here repair,
As to a fane, for praise and prayer.
But say, within its shadowy bounds,
Are such the only sights and sounds
Recorded? Do its annals show
No taint of guilt, no trace of woe?
Ah, me! a story they unfold
Belonging to the days of old,
Which costs sweet Pity to recall
E'en tears of blood, — a martyr's fall!

Why pours the city forth yon countless throng?
For revels gay? No; for the voice of song,
The merry smile, loud laugh, and lusty cheer
Are wanting all, — no sign of joy is there:
Nay, nearer view'd, grief, horror, fear, or ire,
Gives to each face expression dark and dire!
Whether in masses deep they line the way, .
Or form in lesser groups, or singly stray,
One mighty interest, common to them all,
Employs each tongue, or holds each heart in thrall.
What chafes them thus? and whither do they wend
Their moody steps? Near where yon elm doth send
Its boughs on high, as though it did aspire
To pierce the clouds, is rear'd a funeral pyre;

Thither they go, and well each brow and eye,
Gloomy as night, bespeak their sympathy.
Who is the victim? — what the fearful deed
Which asks *such* expiation?   Plead, oh ! plead,
With angel-tongue, sweet Pity, till thou win
A milder doom, how dark soe'er the sin !
Can yonder be the culprit? — he whose brow,
" So saintly bright," no trace of earth doth show
Beyond what Time's rude hand itself has wrought?
His look, his bearing, both forbid the thought ;
For Virtue never did herself such wrong
As trace her lineaments thus clear and strong
On hoary vice; — nay, nay, it cannot be
That he hath lent himself to infamy.
What is the charge alleg'd ?— In that dark time
He liv'd, when Gospel truth was deem'd a crime;
He knew that truth, and taught it, — gently led
The guilty unto Him for guilt that bled;
He won the sinner whilst he chid his deed,
Himself a " living Gospel " all might read.
Such were the crimes that brought him to a death
Which flesh most shrinks from !   But, upheld by faith,
Whilst others weep and tremble as they gaze,
Calmly the scene of torture *he* surveys;

With more than nature's strength then mounts the pyre,
And suffers all the agonies of fire !
A martyr's pangs, a martyr's faith, were his,
And soon — oh, glorious thought ! — a martyr's bliss !

Hail, holy Church ! Say, is it wrong to feel
A glow of pride athwart my bosom steal,
As, one by one, thy glorious martyr-train, —
Who bled, thy rights, thy doctrine to maintain, —
In vision pass before me ? — No ! even pride,
At such a sight, almost is sanctified.
Hail, holy Church ! What though thy leagued foes
The war-cry raise, and round thee fiercely close,
Viewing thy stately towers with jealous eye,
Marking thy bulwarks only to destroy;
What though they long to see thee fall'n — discrown'd —
" Thy pleasant things laid waste," and strewn around ; —
If treachery lurk not in thy hallow'd fold,
If in thy sons, as in their sires of old,
The martyr-spirit live, — if each, if all,
Who bear thy name, do love thy gentle thrall,
Who at thy font, Christ's soldiers sworn and seal'd,
Have never wish'd that sacred vow repeal'd,
But, ever and anon, renew'd the same,
When at thine altar met in His dear name, —

Then, though thy foes be mighty, fear not thou !
The crown shall never fall from off thy brow ;
Thou shalt not o'er thy ravag'd temples mourn,
Nor see " strange fire " upon thy altars burn.
Mother of martyrs ! holy Church ! all hail !
While time itself shall last, thy glory shall prevail !

THE ASH.

FRAXINUS EXCELSIOR.

" The towering ash is fairest in the woods."

SUCH is the testimony of Virgil, — a testimony confirmed by the moderns, who have designated this tree the " Venus of the forest ; " and surely, of all that compose our British sylva, entitled to the rank of *timber* trees, it is decidedly the most elegant.

" All know that in the woods the ash reigns queen,
In graceful beauty soaring to the sky ! "

The same character runs through its various component parts ; thus constituting a beautiful and consistent whole. The easy flowing line of the stem suits the elegant pendent sprays, and these again the bright green slender leaves ; whilst, lastly, the tree itself is in happy accordance with the habitat in which it most delights, — a niche in some grey ruin or splintered rock, where, like the sylvan genius of the scene, it hangs with the most becoming gracefulness.

> " The ash asks not a depth of fruitful mould,
>
> But, like Frugality, on little means
>
> It thrives, and high o'er crevic'd ruins spreads
>
> Its ample shade, or in the naked rock
>
> That nods in air, with graceful limbs depends."

In allusion to this choice of abode Sir Walter Scott says, —

> " Aloft, the ash and warrior oak
>
> Cast anchor in the rifted rock ; "

and Thomson, —

> " Ye ashes wild, resounding o'er the steep."

But, though always apparently most at home in mountainous and rocky scenery, the ash by no means confines itself to such situations, for it grows well in any soil, and abundantly rewards the trouble of the planter. According to Hunter, there are three species of the genus : Fraxinus Ornus, the flowering ash, which yields manna ; Fraxinus americana ; and Fraxinus excelsior, our beautiful common ash, of which the weeping ash is a variety.

Perhaps no tree can boast more legendary renown. From it, if we may credit Hesiod, sprang the brazen race of men. The Edda of Woden gives it similar honour, and moreover describes the gods as sitting in council under its shade. Its inner bark served as a tablet for the scholar : its wood furnished spears for the soldier : —

> " From Pelion's cloudy top, an ash entire
> Old Chiron fell'd, and shap'd it for his sire."

Nay, it has been averred that it formed the missiles in the armoury of Cupid, till, for reasons not stated, it was superseded by the cypress.

Passing by, however, its fabled honours, the real usefulness of the ash is universally acknowledged. Its timber ranks next in value to that of the oak itself, and almost serves as many purposes : —

> ————— " tough-bending ash
> Gives to the humble swain his useful plough,
> And for the peer his prouder chariot builds."

Yet, notwithstanding its beauty and utility, it is frequently denied a place in ornamental plantations, especially in the immediate vicinity of a mansion, on account of the tardiness with which it puts forth its leaves, and its haste in withdrawing them.

The early fading and falling of its foliage may, however, serve as a counterpoise to the prodigality of bloom and of sunshine which frequently characterise

the autumnal months, sometimes even · late in the
season, as though winter were yet afar off. These
diverse appearances of decay on the one hand, and of
vigour on the other, please or offend according to the
mood of the beholder. If his spirits be lively, he is
delighted with every object that " sends a summer
feeling into his heart; " if, on the contrary, they are in
a mournful key, he is disposed to think such autumnal
display as much misplaced as finery on threescore, and
he turns to the withered and falling leaf with a feeling
of secret and sympathising satisfaction.

Though the deep stillness and splendid brightness of
a true autumnal day are, to the writer of these pages, a
source of exquisite enjoyment, there is something even
yet more congenial with her feelings when this season
assumes a garb more suited to the part it has to sustain
in the economy of nature: the herald of universal decay
should surely come, " not trick'd and frounc'd as she is
wont," —

> " But kerchief'd in a comely cloud,
> While rocking winds are piping loud."

Autumn ! this sober guise beseems thee well !
'Tis not for thee to trick thyself like Spring,
Or round thee Summer's sunny vest to fling :
No ! thou must win us by a sadder spell :
Thy voice should ever have a dirge-like swell ;
Thy smile e'er gently mind us of decay :
And if a bird yet sing, oh ! be its lay
Such as might seem of faded flowers the knell !

Now would I seek yon grove of ash, where chief
Thy withering spells seem cast ; and may the sound
Of the dead foliage, as it falls around,
Awake to thoughtfulness, if not to grief.
Not yet " into the sear, the yellow leaf
My May of life has fall'n ; " yet still to me
Nor sound nor sight should e'er unwelcome be,
Which warns me life uncertain is, and brief.

Oh ! Nature, many a lesson could'st thou give
Would man but list thy monitory voice ;
Thou bid'st him pause, and tremblingly rejoice
That he but " lives to die, and dies to live."
May I with reverence meet thy lore receive,
Eloquent teacher ! — yet what fears were mine,

What dark misgivings, did not faith perceive
" A still, small voice " blend other truths with thine,
And, where thou fail'st, take up the wondrous theme,
Till grace and glory on my musings beam!

THE BEECH.

FAGUS SYLVATICA.

"Not a beech but bears some cipher,
Tender word, or amorous text."

To admire the beech, is to rebel against high authority; yet who, that is not entirely devoted to pictorial effect, but must admire it? The oak may excel it in dignity, the elm in beauty, and the ash in gracefulness: still the beech is a noble tree; and in spring, the bright sunny tint of its feathery foliage renders it a most attractive object. Its autumnal livery is also both rich and varied, and harmonises well with the other fading hues of the woods. This even Gilpin allows, who in most other respects has dealt with it so unmercifully. He moreover gives it indirect praise, by admitting it has a *defined* character, which just before he had noticed as "a great source of picturesque beauty." But whilst *he* shows it so little favour, a brother naturalist, White of Selbourne, says, "It is one of the most beautiful and lovely of all the forest trees, whether we consider its stately trunk, its smooth silvery rind, its glossy foliage, or graceful,

spreading, pendulous boughs." It is the very tree for a warm summer's day; for none yields so close a canopy; and beneath its "shady roof," which is not only "star-proof," but sun-proof, the rambler may

> " Sit coolly calm, while all the world without,
> Unsatisfied and sick, tosses in noon."

Virgil praises it especially for this property: in the very opening of his pastorals, he places the tuneful shepherds

> " Where the broad beech an ample shade displays : "

and, indeed, wherever shelter is desirable, the poet generally selects this tree for the purpose :—

> " The sun, from rosy billows risen, had ray'd
>   With gold the mountain tops; when at the foot
> Of a tall beech romantic, whose green shade
>   Fell on a brook, that, sweet-voiced as a lute,
> Through lively pastures wound its sparkling way,
> Sad on the daisied tuft Salicio lay."

> " Under the branches of this beech we flung
> Our limbs at ease, and our bent bows unstrung :
> Thus idly lying, we inspired with zest
> The sweet fresh spirit breathing from the west."

These are sweet summer pictures from " Wiffen's

Garcilasso," to which we subjoin one as beautiful, from
the pen of our own poet Gray: —

> " There at the foot of yonder nodding beech,
> That rears its old fantastic roots on high,
> His listless length at noontide would he stretch,
> And pore upon the brook that bubbles by."

The beech and the chestnut are of the same family.
Hunter and Miller are at variance in their statements
of the number of species which constitute this genus;
the former says three, the latter five: the beautiful
purple beech of our shrubberies is merely a variety. It
is doubted amongst naturalists whether the beech be an
indigenous tree: the uncertainty seems partly grounded
on the assertion of Cæsar, who avers he never saw it in
Britain; but as he says the same of the fir, which is an
undoubted native, those who are jealous of the honour
of their country's sylva may offer this plea for retaining
it amongst our indigenous foresters, and conclude with
Evelyn, that Cæsar's opinion arose " certainly from a
grand mistake; or rather, for that he had not travelled
much up into the country."

From time immemorial the bark of the beech has
been the sylvan tablet of the lover. Shakspeare thus
alludes to the practice, though he does not name the

tree : — " A man haunts our forest that abuses our young trees with carving *Rosalind* upon their bark."

This tender usage has been made a plea, by the poet, for exemption from the woodman's stroke. The plea is eloquently urged, and we only wish it may be the means of sparing many a stately beech from an untimely fall : —

> " Since youthful lovers in my shade
> Their vows of truth and rapture made,
> And on my trunk's surviving frame
> Carv'd many a long-forgotten name ;
> Oh ! by the sighs of gentle sound,
> First breath'd upon this sacred ground ;
> By all that love has whisper'd there,
> Or beauty heard with ravish'd ear ;
> As love's own altar, honour me,
> Spare, woodman, spare the beechen-tree ! "

But though the beech has generally been the depository of the lover's secret, it need not be exclusively his ; affection, in whatever guise it comes, may be allowed the same privilege : shall I then the

> ———— " verse repeat,
> Which lately on the beech's bark I writ ;
> I writ, and sang between ? "

I have been wandering in the wood
   Where wither'd leaves my path were strewing;
And winds, with ire but half subdued,
   Seem'd to a future tempest growing.

Yet, 'mid these symbols of decay,
   My mind was only tun'd to gladness:
And why ? — It is our wedding day ;
   What, then, have I to do with sadness ?

I sat me down beneath a tree, —
   That tree so fam'd for lover's ditty,
When he would try by each fond plea
   To move his mistress' soul to pity.

So smooth the sylvan tablet shone,
   So temptingly 'twas spread before me,
I could not choose but trace thereon,
   No lover's, but a matron's story.

Yet ne'er did Love, when Hope and Youth
   Each minister unto his pleasure,
Feel more of tenderness and truth
   Than I, whilst breathing this fond measure.

    *   *   *   *   *

" Long years ago, and side by side,
    We two were at the altar kneeling;
And whilst on earth the knot was tied,
    Angels, in heaven, our vows were sealing.

Gently thou blamed'st my feeble tone,
    Thou said'st I trembled at the altar;
But had observance deeper gone,
    Thou hadst not said my heart did falter: —

No ! gladly, gladly did I breathe
    The solemn vow to thee which bound me,
And stoop my head for thee to wreathe
    Love's new-wrought fetters close around me.

And thought I, kneeling by thy side,
    Such lot Love's annals ne'er recorded !
Life seem'd all sunshine to the *bride*, —
    What has it to the *wife* afforded?

I will not say, since first we met,
    My path has been all light and glory;
Or, without thorns Love's coronet;
    Or, that no cloud has e'er come o'er me:

D

But oft my fond heart has avow'd
  Those thorns were never of thy twining;
And could thy hand have staid the cloud,
  My sky had e'er been bright and shining:

And as 'twixt midnight clouds afar,
  Some lonely gem is oft seen peeping,
So thy lov'd smile, my bosom's star,
  Has cheer'd me through my night of weeping.

Nor to that smile the *past* alone
  Owes what it hath of joyous seeming;
It is of *present* joys the crown, —
  It is upon the *future* beaming.

I clasp thy ready hand in mine,
  I feel that hand my grasp returning;
'Tis sweet, though mirth may fainter shine,
  That bright as aye Love's lamp is burning!"

THE LIME, OR LINDEN-TREE.

TILIA.

" The stately lime, smooth, gentle, straight, and fair,
(With which no other Dryad can compare.)"

THOUGH we are not prepared, perhaps, entirely to
acquiesce in the sweeping commendation contained in
the closing line of the selected motto, yet can we truly
say the lime is a very beautiful tree: it has an aristocratic
look about it, which makes it a fitting ornament for
cultivated grounds, where we often find it expanding
itself in full glory; it also adorns our woods and hedgerows, for it rejects no soil or situation, though of course
both its size and also the swiftness of its growth depend
a good deal on local circumstances. In rich loamy
ground it grows very rapidly; and this circumstance,
together with the stately beauty of its appearance, makes
it a matter of surprise that it is not more extensively
cultivated: it is objected against it, that the leaf comes
out late, and falls early; but surely this defect is more
than counterbalanced by the properties already men-

tioned; to which may also be added the fragrance of its
pretty, pale flowers, —

————— " at dewy eve
Diffusing odours," —

from which innumerable swarms of bees are seen
" extracting liquid sweets." Besides, as it has been well
remarked, in a paper on trees in Blackwood's Magazine,
— "contrast is one of the finest laws of association; and
bare branches, apart but not repulsive, like some cunning
discord in music, deepens the harmony of the grove."
There are three species of Tilia naturalised in Great
Britain: T. europæa, common lime or linden-tree;
T. grandifolia, or broad-leaved, downy lime; and T.
parvifolia, small-leaved lime: the latter is thought by
some to be really indigenous. The first mentioned, Sir
J. E. Smith says, "is certainly the common lime-tree of
the north of Europe. It is cultivated all over England,
and in many parts of Scotland; and though Ray could
not meet with it indubitably wild, no one can doubt its
being perfectly naturalised. The French, "growing
tired of the horse-chestnut," as Du Hamel reports,
adopted this tree, for ornamental plantations, in the
time of Louis XIV. It generally composes the avenues
of the French as well as English gentry of that date;

and Fenelon, in conformity with this taste, decorates with "flowery lime-trees" his enchanted isle of Calypso.

The grandifolia is the wild lime-tree of Switzerland and the south of Europe, as the europæa is of the north. There are some famous old limes of this species in the churchyard of Sedlitz in Bohemia, which are reported to have miraculously borne hooded leaves, ever since the monks of a neighbouring convent were all hanged upon them.

The lime was of great repute amongst the ancients. It was customary with them to crown themselves with garlands of flowers at their festival, which garlands were bound together with slips of the inner rind of the lime-tree.

Horace thus alludes to it : —

> " Ribands from the linden-tree
> Give a wreath no charms for me."

The specimen delineated was taken from a venerable tree in Matlock parish, which gives the name of Lime-tree Bank to the immediate neighbourhood where it grows. The trunk is quite hollow; but otherwise there is little appearance of decay, as the branches are still vigorous and healthy. "In some writings now in existence, which are six hundred years old, in the possession

of a gentleman who resides at Doncaster, this tree is particularly mentioned, and its site pointed out." *
" Before leaving the lime-tree," says a writer, who seems to know and feel all the pleasures of early reminiscences, " we may notice the delightful associations we have with it, from the recollection of the days of our youth, when, in many an hour of listless idleness, we have sheltered ourselves beneath its impenetrable shade, and, stretched out on the turf below, have listened to the mingled hum of the millions of bees which busily collected the honey from its fragrant flowers; whilst no other sound was heard in the summer air but the occasional sudden, though rare, twitter of the skimming swallow, or the distant cooing of the amorous ringdove; and when all was silent on the earth, save the gentle cropping of the nibbling sheep, or the distant lowing of the kine from the shallows of the river, whither the raging heat had driven them." †

I love the linden-tree!
For it did shade my early home;
And ever when sweet spring did come,

* Rhode's Peak Scenery.
† Sir Thomas Dick Lauder, Bart.

With heart as blithe, as free from care,
As birds that sung and nestled there,
I used to con my book for hours,
Or garlands twine of wilding flowers,
    Beneath the linden-tree.

    I love the linden-tree!
For, oh! when years brought other woes
And other joys than childhood knows,
One summer's eve (so bright a moon
Methought ne'er grac'd the skies of June)
'Twas mine, with beating heart, to hear
The vow to youthful maiden dear,
    Beneath the linden-tree.

    I love the linden-tree!,
Yea, now, when time with sobering hue
Has ting'd the visions fancy drew;
For oft, when meek-eyed eve has given
Her gloom to earth, her star to heaven,
Upward my kindling glance I raise,
And find a fane for prayer and praise
    Beneath the linden-tree.

THE SCOTCH FIR.

PINUS SYLVESTRIS.

" And higher yet the pine-tree hung
His shatter'd trunk, and frequent flung,
Where seem'd the cliffs to meet on high,
His bows athwart the narrow'd sky."

THE exact adaptation of every object in nature to the
situation and circumstances in which it is placed is
beautifully exemplified in the pine tribe. The texture
of their timber, the abundant supply of resinous juices
both in the main stem and the branches, and, above all,
the rigid, needle-shaped leaf, bespeak at once their destiny,—"to dwell aloft amidst the awful palaces of nature,"
to endure the severities of an alpine winter, and to war
with the elements on the mountain and the rock. The
accrose leaf (to use a botanical term), common, with
few exceptions, to those evergreens which usually grow
in northern climates, or on alpine heights, fits them in
·a peculiar manner for braving the difficulties to which
their habitat exposes them, as it allows the snow and

wind free passage through the interstices, securing them alike from an overpowering accumulation of the one, and from the resistless fury of the other. It is also chiefly owing to this peculiar form of the leaves, which do not admit the reflection of much light, that trees of this description wear such a dark, lugubrious appearance; and that, furthermore, by presenting so many points and edges, the wind makes amongst them that " wintry music," so powerfully affecting to the imaginative wanderer, soothing or rousing him, according to the part it sustains in the grand chorus of nature. Burns, with all a poet's feeling, speaks of the enjoyment he experienced from this wild minstrelsy. Whilst listening to its varied cadences on a cloudy winter day, he remarks, " It is my best season for devotion; my mind is wrapt up in a kind of enthusiasm to Him who, in the pompous language of the Hebrew bard, 'walketh on the wings of the wind.' "

The Scotch fir, taking all things into consideration, is esteemed the most valuable of the pines. It grows abundantly in all the countries north of the Baltic, to the seventieth degree of latitude. But it does not confine itself to these parts: it is found on the Carpathian mountains, the Pyrenees, and the Alps; yielding to none of the tribe in the elevation it attains, except the

Pinus uncinata on the Pyrenees, and the Pinus cembra on the Alps.

The testimony of Cæsar goes to disprove its being a native of Britain; its right, however, to be considered such is now placed beyond dispute; the reasons for which are ingeniously and satisfactorily stated in Whitaker's History of Manchester, but are too long to be quoted at large in such a mere sketch as this.

The same desire of brevity will preclude the enumeration of the various species of this extensive genus: but we must single out from the mass the Abies picea, or Norway spruce, as it is considered by some as the great tree of the Alps; — "and so far," says Sir Thomas Dick Lauder, "as our opinion on its effect in landscape may go, we can only say, that with us it is so mentally associated with the grandeur of Swiss scenery, that the sight of it never fails to touch chords in our bosom which awaken the most pleasing recollections. . . What can be more truly sublime," he continues, "than to behold, opposed to the intensely blue ether, the glazed white summits of Mont Blanc or the Jungfrau rising over interminable forests of spruce firs, which clothe the bases of the mountains; while some gigantic specimens rise in groups among the rocks before us, shivered, maimed, and broken by tempests; their dark forms

opposed to all the brilliant hues of some immense gla-
cier." This is a truly alpine picture: we all but see

> ———— " those blasted pines,
> Wrecks of a single winter, barkless, branchless,"

with all the savage, but grand, accompaniments which
he has so vividly sketched.

The Norway spruce, which is but a cultivated tree in
our island, is indigenous in the northern climates of
Europe and Asia; and also, as has been observed, in
the mountain valleys of Switzerland, France, Spain,
and Italy. It is said to attain a greater altitude than
any other European tree, sometimes shooting up to the
height of one hundred and fifty feet. This brings to
mind Milton's sublime description of Satan and his
warlike habiliments. After likening his shield to

> ———— " the moon, whose orb
> Through optic glass the Tuscan artist views
> At evening from the top of Fesolé,"

he continues in the same elevated strain to describe

> " His spear, to equal which the tallest pine
> Hewn on Norwegian hills, to be the mast
> Of some great ammiral, were but a wand."

And again, how finely he borrows the same image, when speaking of the fallen angels : —

> —— " faithful how they stood,
> Their glory wither'd ; as when heaven's fire
> Hath scath'd the forest oaks, or mountain pines,
> With singed top their stately growth, though bare
> Stands on the blasted heath."

Both pines and firs, between which there is a very close alliance, are valuable for a vast variety of purposes. " Sea and land," says Evelyn, " may contend for their many and universal use." The true pine, he adds, was very highly commended for naval architecture : hence the title which Virgil gives it, — " the useful pine for ships ; " and also the many references by our earlier poets to its applicability to marine purposes.

Spenser denominates it

> " The sayling pine ;

and Browne speaks of

> " The pine with whom men through the ocean venture."

They both also share much classical fame; being dedicated, one or both, perhaps indiscriminately, by the ancients to several of their rural deities : they also composed the crown of the victors in the Isthmian games.

But a higher and more honourable distinction belongs to the tribe in the frequent allusions made to it in Holy Writ: the fir, along with the cedar, was used for the planks and beams in the erection of the glorious temple of Solomon. And in many passages it is also associated with that noble tree, in conveying images of prosperity and sublimity.

From the sonorous quality of its wood, it is chosen almost before any other for musical instruments. Even in very early ages its adaptation to such uses was recognised; for we read, when David brought up the ark from the house of Abinadab, he "and all the house of Israel played before the Lord on all manner of instruments made of fir wood; even on harps, and on psalteries, and on timbrels, and on cornets, and on cymbals." It is still used in our days for similar purposes; and, in a fanciful view, there is a strange but beautiful anomaly in this braver of the tempest administering to the devotional and tender emotions of the heart.

Thy throne a rock ! thy canopy the skies !
And, circled in the mountain's·dark embrace,
'Mid what stern pomp thy tow'ring branches rise !
How wild, how lonely is thy dwelling-place !

In the rich mead a God of love we trace,
We feel His bounty in the sun and shower;
But here His milder glories shun our gaze,
Lost in the one dread attribute of power.
I cannot choose but wish thou hadst a fairer bower.

Yet to the scene thy stately form doth give
Appropriate grace; and in thy mountain-hold,
Like flowers with zephyrs " at the shut of eve,"
Thou with the storm hast dallied from of old.
But stateliness of form and bearing bold
Are not thy only boast: there dwells in thee
A soft, sweet spell (if we be rightly told),
Which waiteth but the touch of harmony,
To smooth the brow of care, and make e'en sorrow flee.

Thus be't with me, — when storms of trouble rise,
Which all of woman born, alas! must know,
Built on a rock, and looking to the skies,
Like thee undaunted may I meet the blow.
Not so when call'd to hear of others' woe:
Then may soft pity touch some chord within,
Prompting the tear of sympathy to flow,
And words of healing, such as gently win
The mourner's stricken heart, and pour sweet comfort in.

THE STONE PINE.

PINUS PINEA.

" And still the pine, long-hair'd, and dark and tall,
In lordly right, predominant o'er all."

MOST of the trees of this genus, as has been already
observed, are hardy mountaineers : indeed so associated
are they with alpine scenery, that it would scarcely be
perfect without them. The species under immediate
consideration, however, leaves those inhospitable regions
to the bolder representatives of the clan, and settles itself
in the warm sunny climes of southern Europe. Such
being its usual abode, it does not require those provisions
against the inclemencies of weather which are needful
for the mountain pines; and accordingly we find its
timber is weaker and less resinous, though in other
respects it possesses every distinctive mark common to
the genus to which it belongs, — another proof how
wisely the God of nature varies and proportions his gifts
according to the exigencies of the receiver.

Virgil, with much discrimination, marks this difference

in choice of abode in the pine tribe, only apparently including under the title of *fir* all the hardier species: —

> " The *fir* the *hills*, the ash adorns the woods,
> The *pine* the *gardens*, and the poplar floods."

Gilpin says, that " Italy alone gives birth to the true picturesque pine; where," he adds, " it always suggests ideas of broken porticos, Ionic pillars, triumphal arches, fragments of old temples, and a variety of classic ruins, which in Italian landscape it commonly adorns." This is very true. When imagination dwells on those mighty relics which stand in "ruinous perfection," in so many parts of that classic country, it as invariably associates them with their guardian pine, as it does the rock and the mountain with their proper sylvan accompaniments.

> " A grove springs up through levell'd battlements,
> ' And twines its roots with the imperial hearths."

In perfect unison with its chosen haunts and sombre aspect, are the mournful murmuring sounds which it makes, in common with all acerose-leaved trees, when the wind stirs its boughs: sounds, now loud, now soft, ever varying with the rising or falling breeze. Virgil speaks of " the singing pines." And in another place he says,—

> " The pines of Mænalus were heard to mourn,
> And sounds of woe along the groves were borne."

And Milton, with apparent reference to the readiness with which it responds to the breath of this aërial visitant, says, —

> " His praise, ye winds, that from four quarters blow,
> Breathe soft or loud; and wave your tops, ye pines,
> With every plant — in sign of worship wave."

Many of our modern poets, too, descant most sweetly on this wild natural music; and no marvel, for it is the very poetry of sound.

> ——— " The loud wind through the forest wakes,
> With sound, like ocean's roaring, wild and deep ;
> And in yon gloomy pines strange music wakes,
> Like symphonies unearthly heard in sleep."

It is impossible to read these beautiful poetic descriptions without experiencing something of the feeling which the very objects themselves are calculated to inspire; and it is in this power of abstracting the mind from the common-places of life, and of enabling us to realise the scenes delineated, that the grand spell of

E

poetry consists; and surely when lawfully directed and enjoyed, it constitutes a legitimate source of exquisite pleasure.

But we have wandered from our subject, and must briefly resume it. The stone pine, though mostly associated with Italian scenery, is in some degree naturalised here; the specimens we can show, however, are but poor representatives of those of southern growth. Whether a longer residence amongst us, and due attention to soil and situation on the part of the cultivator, might do something towards restoring its real nobility of character, it remains for time to show; at present, we must look to " Italy alone for the true picturesque pine."

I should have sought thee in some alpine wild,
Upon whose snows bright summer never smil'd,
Cresting the beetling rock, whose dizzy height
Might put to shame the eagle's sunward flight;
And not in fair Italia's sunny plains,
Midst fallen palaces and mouldering fanes.
Ah! why, self-exil'd from thy hardy race,
Mak'st thou in such sad haunts thy dwelling-place?

Com'st thou to mock at ruin? Nay thy mien,
Stately but mournful, suits so well the scene,
I would not deem that in thy hour of prime
Thou cam'st to triumph o'er the wrecks of Time.
No; —rather like the ivy, which has brought
A fairer wreath than sculpture ever wrought,
To hide the breaches Time's rude hand has made,
Oh! let me think thou lend'st thy classic shade,—
Anxious his mighty mischiefs to repair,
And guard and grace the fallen and the fair.

Hadst thou a voice, methinks when eve's still hour
Within us wakes the meditative power,
'Mid scenes like these how sadly sweet 'twould be
To list awhile thy solemn homily;
Thy text these ruins, which do mutely show
What Time, alas! has done, and what can do.
Thou hast a voice.— As from some hidden shrine
I hear thee whisper to this heart of mine;
(This careless heart, which turns so oft away
From aught that seems to mind it of decay;)
Thy theme, Time's changes; and to mortal man,
Whose life's a breath, whose days are but a span,
Whose beauty fadeth as a summer rose,
Methinks no fitter subject couldst thou choose.

Yet stay not here thy monitory strain:
These fallen columns, which bestrew the plain,
But half man's awful destiny suggest, —
Thy changeless leaf may typify the rest.
Time turns whate'er can perish into dust;
Fame, beauty, vigour, each betrays our trust.
But he, the seeming victor, he is doom'd
Himself to fall, in nature's wreck entomb'd;
Whilst the immortal spirit, — thought sublime! —
Alike shall triumph over Death and Time.

THE HOLLY.

ILEX AQUIFOLIUM.

" Oh, Reader ! hast thou ever stood to see
    The holly-tree ?
The eye that contemplates it well perceives
    Its glossy leaves,
Order'd by an intelligence so wise
As might confound the atheist's sophistries.

Below, a circling fence its leaves are seen
    Wrinkled and keen ;
No grazing cattle through their prickly round
    Can reach to wound :
But as they grow where nothing is to fear,
Smooth and unarm'd the pointless leaves appear.

I love to view these things with curious eyes,
    And moralise ;
And in this wisdom of the holly-tree
    Can emblems see
Wherewith perchance to make a pleasant rhyme,
One which may profit in the after time."

IT has been asserted that "nature abhors a vacuum:"
with more truth, judging from the infinite variety every

where observable in her productions, may it be said that nature abhors *sameness*. Take the vegetable world, for instance: what diversity of form, colour, and fragrance; what different means are used for accomplishing similar ends! In one and the same coppice how various in outline and in tint are the trees which compose it! We have just been considering two of the pine genus — evergreens, of course: the holly, too, is an evergreen; but how different in every respect, save *that* from which both derive their general title! Compare the thready, bluish-green leaves of the one, with those of the other, — so "bright with nature's varnish," broad, spinous, and of a warm hue, — and the result will be an acquiescence in the assertion, nature abhors sameness.

The holly is one of the most esteemed of our native evergreens. Its value is felt in sylvan scenery, even in spring and summer, when the woods and thickets are arrayed in the full flush of "leafy luxury;" but it is in connection with the wintry landscape, that it may most confidently challenge our admiration. When all the deciduous trees have "put their graceful foliage off," and "stand barren as lances," the holly cheers us with its unwithering leaf and coral berries, suggesting a thousand images, "pleasant," not "mournful to the soul;" and when its blushing wreaths, as is not

unfrequently the case, are seen shining beneath a
transparent incrustation of frost, they possess a magic
beauty, and look as if they belonged to Fairy-land. The
effect is happily alluded to by Phillips. He, however,
especially names the hawthorn; but the description holds
good with respect to all scarlet-berried trees: —

> " Soon as the silent shades of night withdrew,
> The ruddy morn disclos'd at once to view
> The face of nature in a rich disguise,
> And brighten'd every object to my eyes;
> For every shrub, and every blade of grass,
> And every pointed thorn seem'd wrought in glass:
> In pearls and rubies rich the hawthorns show,
> While through the ice the crimson berries glow."

The holly is a hardy but slow-growing tree. Evelyn,
its most enthusiastic admirer, says on this point, — " True
it is that time must bring this tree to perfection; it does
so to all things else; but," he adds, " we stay seven
years for a tolerable quick: it is worth staying thrice
seven for this, which has no competitor." His rhapsody
on the hedge at Say's Court is too much quoted to need
an introduction here; but it is another proof of the high
estimation in which he held it.

It belongs to a genus containing many species and

varieties. The Ilex aquifolium (our common holly) is indigenous in many countries of the East, in North America, and most parts of Europe. It grows very freely in our island, and gives its name to several places; as Holmesdale, Holmewood, — Holme being one of its vernacular titles.

It is a tree of classical notoriety: Columella recommends it for fences : —

> " A hedge of holly, thieves that would invade
> Repulses, like a growing palisade ;
> Whose numerous leaves such orient greens invest,
> As in deep winter do the spring arrest."

And Virgil places his four contending shepherds

> " Beneath a holm that murmur'd in the breeze."

Thomson mentions it as offering shelter to the birds when they begin to build : —

> " Some to the holly-hedge
> Nestling repair."

It also feeds them in winter with its berries ; but it more than neutralises these friendly offices to the feathered tribe by yielding that glutinous liquid which so often leads to their destruction.

The lines which head this slight sketch refer to the
wise arrangement observable in the different character
of the upper and lower leaves: the latter, in order to
defend it from cattle, &c. being armed with sharp
spines, whilst those which are above the reach of such
depredators "smooth and unarm'd appear."

Is this the grove whose leafy pride
Bright summer's noontide beams defied?
Can yonder be the bank where spring
Did all her store of blossoms fling?
Or this dull stream with leaves o'erstrewn,
The limpid brook, whose silv'ry tone
Seem'd, as its clear waves roll'd along,
The echo of some Naiad's song?
Ah! changing earth! uncertain sky!
How does your glory mock the eye!
Where is it now? — above, beneath,
All, all is torpor, change, and death.
All, said I? Nay, in yonder nook
The holly wears its 'custom'd look,

With berry bright, and leaf ne'er sere,
It greets the "pale declining year;"
A friend, when summer friends do flee,
A "brother for adversity."
But not to fond and faithful breast
Alone does it sweet thoughts suggest;
Oh, no! To thee, whom cares perplex,
Whom troubles fright, whom crosses vex, —
To thee, it speaks in loftier tone,
And breathes a moral all its own.
Come, then, and from the holly tree
Learn what thou art, and what may'st be.
Mark how upon each earthward bough
Edg'd with sharp thorns the leaves do grow,
While those the higher stems that grace
Bear of " the prickly curse" no trace,
As if to teach thee it design'd, —
With earth we leave the thorn behind.

Say thou upon whose brow is set
Care's thorn-entwisted coronet —
Oh! wouldst thou tear it thence, arise
And seek communion with the skies:
The nearer heaven thou soar'st, the less
Shall that keen wreath thy temples press.

If once before thy raptur'd view
Faith open heaven, how faint and few
Will seem all earthly griefs and cares,
Until at last each disappears,
Like thorns from off the leaves which grow
Upon the holly's topmost bough.

THE ASPEN.

POPULUS TREMULA.

" I would not be
A leaf on yonder aspen tree
In every fickle breeze to play
Wildly, weakly, idly gay,
So feebly fram'd, so lightly hung,
By the wing of an insect stirr'd and swung.

Proudly spoken, heart of mine;
Yet weakness and change perchance are thine,
More, and darker and sadder to see,
Than befall the leaves of yonder tree !

Look to thyself, then, ere past is Hope's reign,
And looking and longing alike are in vain ;
Lest thou deem it a bliss to have been, or to be,
But a fluttering leaf on yon aspen tree."

POPLARS, to which genus the aspen belongs, are the
most valuable, says Hunter, of all the aquatics, whether
we consider the quickness of their growth or the magni-

tude to which they will arrive; and though named aquatics, and certainly preferring margins of rivers, and low moist grounds, they will yet thrive exceedingly well in drier situations. It is a class containing many species, three of which — the white, the black, and the trembling poplar — are natives. Amongst those of foreign growth, perhaps the best known, and most distinct in character, is the Lombardy or Po poplar, a native, as its name imports, of Italy, where it grows very plentifully, especially on the banks of the Po. Its towering shape arrests the eye at once, and agreeably breaks the uniformity of outline in our plantations and shrubberies. It has also another beauty peculiar to itself; and that is, as Gilpin observes, "the waving line it forms when agitated by the wind. Most trees in this circumstance are partially agitated: one side is at rest, while the other is in motion; but the Italian poplar waves in one simple sweep from the top to the bottom."

—— " The poplar's shoot,
That like a feather waves from head to foot."

For this graceful addition to our sylva we are indebted to the Earl of Rochford, who brought it hither in the year 1758, so that it is comparatively of recent introduction; but our climate suits it so well, that already it may be considered as completely naturalised.

The poplar tribe shares, in common with many other trees, the distinction of a classical origin. The ancient poets averred that the weeping sisters of " the temerarious Phaëton " were transformed into poplars. Virgil, however, gives this honour to the alder.

But we must not wander too long from our main subject, the aspen or trembling poplar, which is not only indigenous in our island, but a native of Europe from Sweden to Italy. It is a tree of quick growth, readily springing up in any soil or situation, and sometimes attaining the height of ninety feet. From the tremulousness of its leaves it has derived its name, and has also become a " by-word and a proverb." Amongst the wild glens of the Highlands, fit nurseries for superstitious fancies and traditionary legends, it is a current notion that the cross was made of this tree, and that therefore its leaves can never rest. To the philosopher, science offers a more satisfactory solution of the problem. "To the compression of the petiole," says Drummond, "we are chiefly to attribute the tremulous or turning motion of the leaves of this tree. The compression is chiefly at the end next the leaf; and as it is vertical, while the position of the leaf is horizontal,

the slightest breath of wind throws the latter into
agitation."

———————

Daylight is closing, but the west
   Still with the pomp of sunset glows,
And crimson cloud on mountain's breast,
   And tower, and spire, its radiance throws,
While one by one in eastern skies
" The stars which usher evening rise."

How deep, how holy is the calm !
   Each sound seems hush'd by magic spell,
As if sweet Peace her honied balm
   Blent with each dewdrop as it fell;
And Zephyrus, in tranc'd repose,
Slept on the bosom of the rose.

(Would that the cares which vex the breast
   Of man, and aye his steps pursue,
Had, too, an evening hour of rest,
   A pause like this of Nature knew !
Alas ! there's that in his dark lot
Which such sweet influence toucheth not.)

Yet in this deep tranquillity,
   When e'en the thistle's down is still,
Trembles yon towering aspen tree,
   Like one whose bygone deeds of ill,
At hush of night, before him sweep,
   To scare his dreams and " murder sleep."

Far off in Highland wilds 'tis said
   (But Truth now laughs at Fancy's lore),
That of this tree the cross was made
   Which erst the Lord of Glory bore,
And of that deed its leaves confess
E'er since a troubled consciousness.

We boast of clearer light; but say,
   Hath Science, in her lofty pride,
For every legend swept away
   Some better, holier truth supplied?
What hath she to the wanderer given
To help him on his road to heaven?

Say, who hath gaz'd upon this tree
   With that strange legend in his mind,
But inward turn'd his eye to see
   If answering feeling he could find,—

A trembling for that guilt which gave
His Saviour to the cross and grave?

And who such glance did·inward bend,
  But scorn'd the apathy and pride
Which make him slight that more than friend,
  For him who bled, for him who died;
Nor pray'd his callous heart might prove
What 't is to tremble, weep, and love?

THE BIRCH.

BETULA ALBA.

" I find myself
Beneath a weeping birch (most beautiful
Of forest trees, the lady of the woods)."

THIS sketch of the birch is not less correct than it is
poetical. There is an elegance in its general appearance
which fully justifies the poet's fancy, and entitles it to
the appellation he has given it, of "lady of the woods."
In every. season, and under all circumstances, it is a
lovely object; nothing can exceed the tender hue of its
vernal leaves, as they wave to and fro in the sunshine.
In summer, perhaps, it loses something of its beauty, as
its bright tints then subside into a more sober green;
still it preserves its gracefulness of aspect. In autumn it
almost more than regains what it lost in summer; whilst
winter, which deprives most other vegetable productions
of their charms, by displaying more fully the slight
silvery stem and delicate ramifications of the birch,
seems but to invest it with new attractions.

Notwithstanding its fragility of appearance, the birch is a most hardy tree, refusing no soil or situation, however unpromising: indeed, two of the species — the dwarf birch, Betula nana, and the hoary alder, Betula incana — will grow where scarcely any thing else will, approaching nearer the arctic pole than any other tree, except the dwarf willow. That diminutive species of birch, Betula nana, has lately been discovered in the Highlands, where a strange and superstitious notion is prevalent accounting for its stunted growth, which they imagine is owing to its having furnished the rod with which Christ was scourged.

To the inhabitants of finely-timbered countries, the birch, distinct from considerations of pictorial effect, is a tree of small value; but to such as dwell in high latitudes, it is inestimable, holding, in their regard, the same rank in the vegetable kingdom as the rein-deer does in the animal. Of its wood they form those light canoes, which answer every purpose of their limited navigation; its bark furnishes them with an almost impenetrable roof for their huts, and is ingeniously converted into various articles of clothing, whilst its inner coat, dried and ground, is a substitute for flour in times of scarcity; its sap affords them a refreshing beverage; its branches yield them fuel; and its leaves "form a soft elastic couch for the cradle of infancy."

The birch is a beautiful appendage to mountainous and rocky scenery, where it may often be observed springing out of some tiny fissure, retaining its footing by so slight a hold that it seems hanging in air. It is truly a Scottish tree; and as such, with great propriety, Sir W. Scott gives it a place in his graphic description of Highland scenery : —

> " With boughs that quaked at every breath,
> Grey birch and aspen wept beneath."

How frequently, too, is it introduced into the poetry of Burns, and under what alluring denominations, — " the gay green birk," " the fragrant birk !"

> " Down by the burn, where *scented birks*
> Wi' dew are hanging clear."

" The birks of Aberfeldy," indeed, are almost as duly immortalised by his little sprightly song bearing that title, as even the " mountain daisy" itself by the pathetic stanzas he has addressed to it. It has been remarked, that " the very smell of the first springing leaves of this tree wonderfully recruits and exhilarates the spirits." Whether this effect be really produced by physical causes, or merely by the power of association, others must decide; perhaps both lend their aid in bringing about so pleasant a result. There is a variety, which, from the pensile character of its foliage, is denominated " the weeping birch." We are here reminded of a glowing passage, in the article on trees before referred to, denying the applicability of such an epithet to any thing in inanimate nature. " That stem, white as silver and smooth as silk, seen so straight in the green sylvan light, and thus airily overarching the coppice with lambent tresses, such as fancy might picture for the mermaid's hair, is said by us, who vainly attribute our own sadness to unsorrowing nature, to belong to a tree that *weeps ;* though a weight of joy it is, and of exceeding gladness, that thus depresses her pendant beauty till it droops, as we think, like that of a being overcome with grief." We are glad the eloquent writer does not quarrel with Fancy, for attributing to inanimate objects feelings and passions in common with sentient beings, but merely with this particular appropriation of them. His creed, perhaps, is — " In nature there is nothing melancholy;" yet, as uninterrupted happiness is not the lot even of the most favoured of mortals, we rob Nature of her dearest charm of companionship, if we may not call upon her to sympathise with us in sorrow as well as in joy.

O ! come to the meadows, the meadows are gay,
The green grass is springing, the lambs are at play;
To a zephyr the rude blast has sunk, and its sigh
Has awaken'd the daisy to gaze on the sky:
    Earth smileth in gladness,
    And sorrow and sadness
Have fled with dark winter, — away then, away !

O ! come to the glen, where the bright silver rill,
Like a newly freed captive, is roaming at will;
Uncertain alike both its mood and its course,
Now softly 'tis singing, now murmuring hoarse;
    Now winding in error,
    Now calm as a mirror
For Fay or for Dryad, it rests and is still.

O ! come to the woodlands, 'tis joy to behold
The new-waken'd buds in our pathway unfold;
For spring has come forth, and the bland southern breeze
Is telling the tale to the shrubs and the trees,
    Which, anxious to show her
    The duty they owe her,
Have deck'd themselves gaily in em'rald and gold.

How tender, yet bright, is the tint that is flung
O'er each delicate spray, which so lightly is hung,
    That, like breeze of the mountain,
    . Or gush of the fountain,
It owns not of rest or of slumber the thrall.

Yet 't is said that in climes o'er the far northern sea,
Of its sweet-scented leaves, though so restless they be,
The mother a couch for her infant doth spread;
And sure, while she sings by his soft leafy bed,
    And watcheth his slumbers,
    The theme of her numbers
Is — the gem of the forest, the bonnie birch-tree.

THE COMMON ALDER.

ALNUS GLUTINOSA.

————— " From out the cavern'd rock,
In living rills a gushing fountain broke;
Around it and above, for ever green,
The bushing alders form'd a shady scene."

THE alder loves to make its home " beside all waters;"
the clear lake, the sedgy pool, the majestic river, " the
crisped brook,"—all are alike to it. Wherever there is
water, there, almost to a certainty, shall we find the
alder.

By sylvan connoisseurs the alder is considered the
most picturesque of the aquatic tribe, except the weeping
willow. But it is not a mere beautifier of that description
of scenery to which it chiefly confines itself; it forms a
strong natural embankment against the encroachments
of the current; and it is also said, in common with most
other trees that love the stream, to possess properties
for correcting the unhealthy air peculiar to such situations, in a much greater degree than those which grow
in places of less humidity.

It is curious to mark, in the same genus, what diversity is sometimes exhibited in the mode of growth, peculiar habits, and choice of abode of the different species. Whilst Alnus glutinosa (our common alder) shows such decided preference for river scenery, the hoary or silver-leaved alder quits the valley for the mountains, and grows at an elevation of 6000 feet above the level of the sea. A stunted growth is the consequence of its ambitious propensities; for whilst the former attains a height of from thirty to forty feet, the latter is a mere shrub, its main stem being scarcely thicker than the human arm.

According to Linnæus, the birch and the alder are joined in the same genus. They differ widely in their general aspect, the birch being remarkable for the elegance of its form and the delicate tint of its foliage; whilst the alder sometimes "puts on so much of the bold resolute character of the oak, that it might be mistaken for that tree, but for the intense depth of its green hue." It serves a variety of purposes. Immersed in water it becomes exceedingly hard; and, on that account, was used by the ancients, and is still used by the moderns, to form a foundation for buildings erected in swampy situations. In the infancy of navigation it was employed by them in the construction of their vessels. In reference to which Virgil says, —

" When hollow alders first the waters tried."

And again, —

" And down the Po the rapid alders glide."

In the following passage he considers it as an emblem
of friendship : —

" Gallus, my much belov'd ! for whom I feel
The flame of purest friendship rising still ;
So by a brook the verdant alders rise,
When fostering zephyrs fan the vernal skies."

What additional zest does this play of fancy give to a
country ramble ! There are some who value trees only
for their timber or their shade; there are others to
whom they suggest a thousand varied images, — some
pleasurable, some perhaps painful, but all interesting.
They hear them,

" As they bow their hoary heads, relate,
In murmuring sounds, the dark decrees of Fate ;
While visions, as poetic eyes avow,
Cling to each leaf, and swarm on every bough."

Trees that, like the alder, follow the stream, and hang
over it with seeming fondness, offer many such associations: viewed in one light, they appear the types of

a grovelling nature; thus Coleridge regarded them.
"Shall man," says he, "alone stoop? shall his pursuits
and desires, the reflections of his inward life, be like
the reflected image of a tree on the edge of a pool, that
grows downward, and seeks a mock heaven in the un-
stable element beneath it, in neighbourhood with the
slim water-weeds and oozy bottom-grass, that are yet
better than itself and more noble, in as far as sub-
stances that appear as shadows are preferable to shadows
mistaken for substance?"

To others they present an image of gratitude.

But the most familiar and the most pleasing idea
they can suggest is that of friendship. Virgil, as we
have already observed, regarded the alder in this point
of view; other authors, also, have treated it in the same
manner, and indeed it is an idea which would naturally
and readily occur to the most unimaginative mind.

I know a nook just meet for Dryad's bower,
So pleasant 't is, and leafy; not a flower
That loves the shade is wanting, not a tree,
From the light birch that springs so airily,
To the wide-spreading beech and giant oak,
Whose massy shade no sunbeam ever broke.

But chiefly there the alder, darkly green,
In such fix'd attitude doth fondly lean
O'er the clear brook, as 't would not lose one tone
Of its sweet parley as it murmur'd on;
And then, what time the soft winds gently stirr'd
Its darkling leaves, it too would breathe some word
Of answering kindness.   Ah! in by-gone hours,
When Fancy, proud to try her new-born powers,
From all she heard or saw stole some sweet thought,
Oft has that tree some theme for musing brought.
If harsh of mood, too hardly would she deem
'T was in self-homage bending o'er the stream,
Like Beauty o'er her mirror, pleased to find
Its image in that glassy stream enshrined.
Anon, repenting of a thought so rude,
'T would seem to her the type of gratitude,
Shading the brook that fed it, lest the sun
In mid career should gaze too fierce thereon.
And then a softer image it supplied,
For ever bending o'er that crystal tide,
For ever list'ning to its liquid chime,
Though all the sounds and sights of summer time —
A sky all glory, and an earth all bloom,
Gales breathing only music and perfume —

Seem'd all intent to win its love; but, no —
It mark'd alone that streamlet's gentle flow.

Once ('tis long since) when Fancy thus had been
Framing sweet visions in that leafy scene,
I took my lyre, and bade each answering chord
Its silence break, her musings to record.
I was a mourner then; I wept the dead;
Yea, some I lov'd were not, and I had said —
Too rashly said! — that joy would ne'er relume
A heart whose hopes were buried in the tomb.
Sad was my lay at first; but as I pour'd
My feelings forth, my spirit seem'd restor'd
To wonted calmness, for I thought the while
On one whose gentle voice and kindly smile
Were mine, still mine. I touch'd my harp again,
Less sadly than before — and such my strain: —

And, said I, joy's bright sun had set,
  No more to gild my path of shade!
Well, on eve's dewy coronet
  Shine moon and star when sunbeams fade
Then will I not desponding grieve,
  Though dim my future path may be,
For such as are those lights to eve
  Shall be thy smile of love to me.

And, said I, joy's gay flowers no more
  Will grace such sunless heart as mine !
Well, be it so — the *sweetest* flower
  Not oft in gaudy tints doth shine.
The wild rose on the storm-beat rock
  Than garden queen I 'd rather see,
And such, mid sorrow's tempest-shock,
  Yea, such is now thy love to me.

When musing on the dead, my eye
  Half wistful turns to holier sphere;
I think of thee, and feel a tie
  Still sweetly hold me captive here.
Should that too break — oh ! then most lone,
  Most desolate my heart would be;
My bosom's evening star were gone,
  And lost life's sweetest flower to me.

Yon alder leaning o'er the brook
  Methinks doth type of love supply;
Above, around, nought wins its look
  From the clear stream that murmurs by.
And thus, when thou art near, I seem
  To have no thought for aught but thee; —
Thou art the star, the flow'r, the stream,
  The all of earthly joy to me.

THE WEEPING WILLOW.

" By the rivers of Babylon, there we sat down; yea, we wept, when
we remembered Zion.

" We hanged our harps upon the willows in the midst thereof."

AFTER contemplating the solemn sadness of this touching picture, drawn by the pen of inspiration, every other
association connected with the willow must not only
appear insipid, but almost impertinent; except, indeed,
such as may be borrowed from the same hallowed
source.

Every production of nature alluded to in the Bible
is at once invested with a sacred character, and possesses an indescribable interest. It is this which gives
the willow a claim on our regard, very far beyond
what it might derive from the graceful effect of its
drooping boughs, or, indeed, from any other quality by
which it is distinguished. At the Feast of Tabernacles,
when, in commemoration of their fathers' dwelling in
tents during their forty years' sojourn in the wilderness,

the Israelites were commanded to dwell in booths made of " goodly trees, and rejoice before the Lord their God seven days;" those selected for the occasion were " branches of palm trees and willows of the brook:" to which Nehemiah adds branches of olive, pine, and myrtle. These, being all tied together with gold and silver strings, were carried in procession by the people during the feast. This festival was further designed as a solemn acknowledgment of the mercy of God, "who crowneth the year with his goodness," on the ingathering of the various fruits of the earth.

The Latin name Salix, signifying to spring up, well describes the rapid growth of the willow tribe. This characteristic, as well as its choice of situation, is beautifully alluded to in Isaiah, xliv. 4.: — " They shall spring up as among grass, as willows by the water-courses." Not fewer than one hundred and forty-one different species of Salix have been enumerated by Sir James E. Smith. The one denominated Salix Babylonica, (our English weeping willow) is a native of the Levant, the coast of Persia, and other places in the East. The manner of its introduction into England is curious: the account is as follows : — Pope, the celebrated poet, having received a present of Turkey figs, observed a twig of the basket in which they were packed, putting out a

shoot. This twig he planted in his garden; it soon became a fine tree, and from it all our weeping willows
have descended. This particular tree was felled in 1801;
a circumstance which one cannot help regretting. The
Salix babylonica is generally planted by a still pool, to
which it is a beautiful and appropriate ornament; and
when, in misty weather, drops of water are seen distilling
from the extremities of its branches, nothing can be more
descriptive than the title it has obtained of weeping
willow.

In ages past, where Babel's mighty waters
   Roll'd darkly onward, sat a weeping band,
Poor remnant of proud Judah's sons and daughters,
   Captives and exiles from their father-land.

And while their tears they mingled with the billow,
   And while their foes the bitter taunt still flung,
" Sing us the songs of Zion," — on the willow
   Their silent harps with mournful meaning hung.

And e'er since then, that tree so sadly waving
　By the still gliding stream, or plashy spring,
Whether suns brighten or dark storms are raving,
　" Seems link'd to sorrow like a holy thing; "

And still it offers to the broken-hearted
　The friendly covert of its drooping bough.
Oh well it were, meek tree, when joy's departed,
　If man like thee could bend him to the blow!

THE MOUNTAIN ASH, or ROWAN TREE.

PYRUS AUCUPARIA.

——— " The mountain ash
No eye can overlook, when mid a grove
Of yet unfaded trees she lifts her head,
Deck'd with autumnal berries, that outshine
Spring's richest blossoms; and ye may have mark'd
By a brook side or solitary tarn,
How she her station doth adorn · the pool
Glows at her feet, and all the gloomy rocks
Are brighten'd round her."

THE common appellation of this beautiful tree, the character of its foliage, and its choice of situation, have led to some confusion respecting its classification. Gerarde and Gilpin, for instance, have considered it a variety of the true ash (Fraxinus); an error which has not escaped the animadversions of later botanists, who all now concur in comprehending it in the genus Pyrus.

It is a tree of slow growth; the wood is compact and tough, which made it, in the days of our warlike ancestors of some repute for bows: but now it is not so much cultivated for the sake of utility, as for ornament.

It is very hardy, and will flourish in any soil or situation; but it prefers the mountain to the valley, and it is in wild alpine districts that we must look for it in perfection: —

> " There clings the rowan to the rock,
>   And through the foliage shows its head,
>   With narrow leaves and berries red."

In these, its favourite haunts, it continually presents itself to the eye of the traveller. Sometimes it is seen adorning the side of a rugged mountain; sometimes rising from a rock

> ———— Amid the brook,
>   Grey as the stone to which it clings, half root
>   Half trunk; "

and now, overshadowing a Highland hut, —

> " Some three strides up the hill a mountain ash
>   Stretches its lower boughs and scarlet clusters
>   O'er the old thatch."

When found in such a habitat, we may shrewdly suspect it has been planted there by the hand of super-

stition; for the simple mountaineers, both in Scotland and
Wales, believe that in the neighbourhood of this tree

> ———— " No evil thing that walks by night
> In fog or fire, by lake or moorish fen,
> Blue meagre hag, or stubborn unlaid ghost
> That breaks his magic chains at curfew time, —
> No goblin, or swart fairy of the mine,
> Hath hurtful power."

Cattle were imagined to be especially indebted to
its protecting spells. Formerly it was no uncommon
sight to see a herd grazing each with a sprig of mountain ash fastened with red tape to its left horn; and
still the Scottish dairy-maid drives her cattle to the
summer pastures with a twig of rowan.*

Its reputed abhorrence of the whole brood of ne-
cromancers, male and female, makes it appear a somewhat inappropriate material for the sacrificial pile of
that mysterious personage, half monk, half wizard, so

* The same beneficent influence was supposed to extend also to the
human species, as the following passage from " The Monastery " goes to
prove : — " I have tied red tape round the bairnes' throats, and given
ilk ane o' them a riding wand of rowan tree, forby sewing up a slip of
witch elm in their doublets, and I wish to know of your reverence if
there be ony thing mair that a lone woman can do in the matter of ghaists
and faeries ? "

pictorially described by Sir Walter Scott in " The Lady of the Lake: " —

> " A heap of wither'd boughs was piled,
> Of juniper and rowan wild,
> Mingled with shivers from the oak,
> Rent by the lightning's recent stroke."

It is curious to observe kindred superstitions obtaining in climes far distant from each other, amongst people differing as widely as possible in appearance, manners, and laws. We have an instance of this recorded by the late excellent Bishop Heber. He states, that meeting with a species of mimosa very like the mountain ash, he could not forbear staying awhile to examine it; when, seeing him so employed, a native came up to him, and informed him that that tree was a security against magic, and that no wizard could come within its shade.

The mountain ash was much esteemed by the Druids, in proof of which it is found more frequently in the neighbourhood of druidical circles than any other tree. We should scarcely have expected this from the character it has since borne. Its connection (in what way we know not) with their mystic rites renders it but an inappropriate appanage of a Christian burial-ground, yet in Wales it is almost as commonly found in that sacred enclosure as the yew; and in by-gone times, on one particular day in the year, the Welsh peasantry wore a cross made of its wood.

These superstitious notions and observances are fading fast away, except in very remote places; and it is most desirable they should do so, for we would not have Reason surrender herself hoodwinked to Credulity. Yet the imaginative mind will, at times, have its own regrets that the dale, the mountain, and the forest, should thus become stripped of their legendary lore, and will enter into the feelings which prompted the poet to ask, somewhat reproachfully, —

> ——— " Do not all charms fly
> At the mere touch of cold philosophy ?
> There was an awful rainbow once in heaven, —
> We know her woof, her texture, she is given
> In the dull catalogue of common things.
> Philosophy will clip an angel's wings,
> Conquer all mysteries by rule and line,
> Empty the haunted air, and gnomed mine,—
> Unweave a rainbow."

Thanks to thee, Memory! we do owe thee much,
   Thou faithful chronicler of by-gone years;
Yea, though thou sometimes wakest by sudden touch
   " Thoughts which do lie almost too deep for tears;"
For many a pleasure hast thou hoarded too,
   And when the present on the sense doth pall,
When Hope no longer gilds the distant view,
   Then dost thou, Memory, some sweet scene recall, —
Not dimm'd, but soften'd by those clouds which cast
A magic twilight round each vision of the past.

The past! ah, who would with its records part,
   Because that some are blotted with a tear?
The smiles which made sweet sunshine in the heart,
   The tones that were as music to the ear,
" The scenes where erst our careless Childhood stray'd,"
   Or those which Youth's more fervid pleasures shared:
Oh! ne'er may dark Oblivion's spells be laid
   On aught so loved, so sacred, so endear'd:
Let not one look, one tone, one scene be lost,
Though many a tender tear the sweet remembrance
    cost.

And other joys thou hast— a motley train —
   Wherewith to while away a vacant hour;

Perchance they hold us by a slighter chain,
   Yet the heart owns their fascinating power.
To those, whom Nature's sacred joys delight,
   Oh! what sweet visions, Memory, canst thou bring,
Of stream, of valley, or of wood-crown'd height,
   Now in morn's pearly lustre glistening,
Now in the full broad glare of noon arrayed,
And now half hid from view in evening's purple
     shade.

Oh! to hold converse with the whispering trees, —
   To list the brooklet's sweet continuous chime,
The varying cadence of the evening breeze,
   Or "song of early birds" at matin-time:
To view the first fair buds of Spring unclose,
   Or youthful Summer round her laughing brow
With looks of triumph twine the first wild rose, —
   To view rich Autumn bend with fruit each bough,
Or ev'n stern Winter's desolate array,
His dazzling robe of snow, and frost-incrusted spray!

Now, Memory, do thine office, — disenthral
   From present sights and sounds mine eye and ear:
To this some native melody recall,
   To that some sunny landscape passing fair.

Pent in a town, where never yet the sky
   Wore its own azure, or where yet the sun
Unsullied rose, lift but before mine eye
   Thy magic mirror, and these vapours dun
Shall roll away, and to my glance be given
Woods, vales, and meads, outspread beneath a cloudless
      heaven.

One effort more, and now I seem to stand
   On proud Helvellyn, — feel around me blow
The keen, fresh breeze; or tread " the silver strand "
   Of the blue lake, and watch its gentle flow:
Now pierce the glen where Ayrey's * torrent boils,
   And mark the sunbeams dally with the spray,
Till o'er the troubled flood an iris smiles,
   As if to charm its wrathful mood away;
Or pitying view each little flower, bright-hued,
Weeping its life away in sunless solitude.

---

* Ayrey, or Ara-force, is one of the most picturesque waterfalls in the
lake district. In its descent it flings up clouds of spray, which, when
touched by the sun, form beautiful miniature rainbows. After pursuing
its troubled course 'through a romantic glen, whose rocky walls are
overhung with native wood, amongst which the mountain ash is con-
spicuously beautiful, it empties itself into Ullswater.

Now glancing upward to a dizzy height,
  I see the rowan fling its feathery sprays
O'er the cleft rocks, with scarlet fruit so bright,
  It seems a sylvan iris to my gaze.
Fairest of trees that love the rushing stream,
  The rocky glen, or mountain's shaggy side !
Ah ! well, methinks, of yore might Fancy deem
  No evil thing could in thy presence bide ;
So pure thou look'st, so fearless, and so free,
Owning no spells thyself save beauty's witchery.

But hark ! stern duty calls ; — sweet dreams, farewell !
  I may no longer tread the winding glen,
But quit its lonely charms, its torrents' swell,
  For dingy streets, " and busy hum of men."
Well, be it so : — though all without be drear,
  Within my home at least is peace and rest.
Methinks the lark that springs the dawn to cheer
  Did never yet turn sorrowing to his nest ;
No ! though he sings while soaring, — yet his strain
Is blythest when he nears his lowly home again.

THE WILD CHERRY.

PRUNUS CERASUS.

" See, Nature hastes her earliest wreaths to bring
With all the incense of the breathing spring."

" WHAT are those living hills of snow, or of some substance purer in its brightness even than any snow that falls, and fades in one night, on the mountain-top? Trees are they, fruit trees — the wild cherry: and can that be a load of blossoms? Fairer never grew before poet's eye of old in the fabled Hesperides. See, how what we call snow brightens into pink*, yet still the whole glory is white !"

What woodland wanderer will say this description, glowing as it is, is overcharged? He who has once seen this beautiful tree, covered with pearly blossoms, relieving with its lighter graces the massy foliage of the forest, will be rather tempted to think that no description can

---

* The full-grown blossoms are *perfectly white*, but the buds have a faint tinge of pink; the calyx and stem also exhibit stronger shades of the same colour, so that at a distance the appearance of the trees justifies the above description.

do it justice. So truly does it breathe of spring, that if he be in a mood to "find tongues in trees," it reminds him more emphatically, perhaps, than any of its sylvan companions, that "the winter is past, the rain is over and gone, the flowers appear on the earth, the time of the singing birds is come, and the voice of the turtle is heard in our land." Nor is it only when thus blended with heavier trees that its value is chiefly felt; it may, perhaps, even more confidently challenge our admiration when it is seen, as it frequently is, softening the rugged features of the north, decorating some rocky precipice or mountain torrent. There are some very fine specimens of the wild cherry in the neighbourhood of our English lakes, especially near Rydal water; one or two of which measure seven or eight feet in circumference near the ground, and rise to a proportionable height.

Our native cherries, of which there are but two species, Prunus cerasus, and Prunus padus, belong to a very comprehensive genus, consisting for the most part of cultivated species, which, besides adorning our orchards with their blossoms, yield also delicious fruit for our table. Apricots, and the various kinds of plums, are comprised in this class, as well as the wild and garden cherry.

The latter was first brought to Rome from Pontus by Lucullus, after the Mithridatic war: a cherry-tree, laden with fruit, was borne in procession at his triumph; and, according to Sir William Temple, within the space of a hundred years, it travelled westward with the Roman conquests, till at last it gained a footing in Britain. Some writers, however, affirm that it did not make its appearance amongst us till the reign of Henry the Eighth, giving the honour of its introduction to Richard Haines, fruiterer to that monarch; but the remains of aged cherry-trees, still visible in some of the old abbey gardens, make its earlier cultivation probable. If Pliny is to be trusted, we shall find his account verifies the first-mentioned date; for he says positively, "In less than one hundred and twenty years after the conquest of Pontus, other lands had cherries, even as far as Britain, beyond the ocean." Towards the middle of the sixteenth century, cherries were so common as to be hawked about in the metropolis: it was customary to indicate the commencement of the season by carrying a bough laden with this tempting fruit through the streets and alleys. The author, whose essay on gardening we have just quoted, mentions cherries and apples, as "of all other fruits, the most innocent food:" some may be tempted to question this high authority, and to doubt whether he really has made the best possible selection.

Shakspeare names the cherry in one or two of his plays; thus, in Henry the Eighth, —

> —— " 'Tis as like you
> As cherry is to cherry."

And again, in the Midsummer Night's Dream, Helena, describing the close friendship subsisting between herself and Hermia, says, —

> —— " So we grew together
> Like to a double cherry; seeming parted,
> But yet a union in partition."

Nor was the beautiful ruby tint of its fruit forgotten by the lover when he would sing his lady's praises: —

> " Her lippes soft and mery
> Emblomed like the chery."

And, moreover, not only did its fruit furnish him with a comparison when he would extol her beauty, but its bark also supplied him with a tablet whereon to transcribe his admiration; at least, so says Evelyn. Such are his words: " These pretty monuments of courtship, I find, were much used on the cherry-tree (I suppose the wild one), which has a very smooth rind : —

> " Repeat ; thy words on cherry-bark I'll take,
> And that red skin my table-book will make."

The fruit of the wild cherry, though so beautiful to the eye, is harsh and crude to the taste: it has been suggested that cultivation might remedy this evil, and change its uninviting properties to that delicious flavour which distinguishes the garden species. But who, merely to gratify the palate, would willingly allow it to undergo any transmutation, lest the native gracefulness of the tree should be impaired? for no cultivated species can exceed, or even equal, it in beauty. This, as we have before intimated, may be rendered more attractive, by comparison with the scenes in which we most commonly find it: it does not, like orchard trees, add "sweets to the sweets," but "gives its beauties to the wilderness," and maketh

> ———— " Gay the solitary place,
> Where no eye sees it."

Lovely, however, as are its blossoms, they are, like most lovely things — short lived; if they do not "come up in a night, and perish in a night," yet their days are

numbered: they bud, bloom, and die in less than a
fortnight. Their very frailty, however, has immortalised
them in the following touching lines by Herrick: —

> " Ye may simper, blush, and smile,
> And perfume the air awhile,
> But, sweet things, ye must be gone ;
> Fruit, ye know, is coming on :
> Then, ah! then, where is your grace,
> When as cherries come in place?"

Season of hope and promise! art thou come, —
Come with thy changeful looks, thy smiles and tears,
Thy angry sallies, and relentings kind?
I welcome thee, capricious as thou art;
Nay, oft I think thy very waywardness
Adds but more sweetness to thy gentler moods.
How have I long'd for thee! how watch'd each sign
Which show'd me of thy coming — from the hour
When the pale snowdrop, ever in the van
Of floral heralds, caught my gladden'd view,
Till now, when woods, and meads, and bowers, full-rob'd,
Proclaim thee in the zenith of thy power!

H

Oh what a world of beauty ! Summer's bloom
And Autumn's matron pride — say what are they,
Compar'd with thee, thou Hebe of the year?
As far thy budding graces theirs excel
As hope exceeds enjoyment, in a world
That never yielded half the promis'd bliss.
Look at these flowers, just peeping from their nest
Of moss and leaves, so beautifully shy —
It may be that the sight as yet is new,
Or else, methinks, I love these lowly ones
More than the rose herself; and better far
Than boughs with fruitage crown'd, the dazzling wreaths
Which deck yon wilding cherry, — white as snow,
Save where a faint soft blush, all but invisible,
Steals o'er the whiteness, as if Nature felt
Uncertain of the effect, and fear'd to mar
What seem'd already perfect.   As I gaze
With kindling glance upon a scene so fair,
Like some fond mother, who, while she doth watch
The placid slumbers of her cradled babe,
Forgets, ah, bitter thought ! man's doom of ill, —
So I forget a curse yet unrepeal'd,
All lovely as she looks, on Nature lies, —
That all above, around me, and beneath,
Earth, sea, and sky, despite their present calm,

Obnoxious are to change, and blight, and storm,
As man to sin and death.

Remembrance sad!
And yet, though sad, sweet thoughts 'twill prompt at
     times;
For if a *fallen* world be still so fair, —
A world which sin has marr'd, where sin doth dwell, —
Oh! what will be that paradise of God
Prepar'd for those who love Him! Eye nor ear
Hath seen or heard the glory. There no blight,
No change of season comes, for sin is not;
But God himself will be the light thereof,
" And one unbounded spring encircle all."

THE YEW.

TAXUS BACCATA.

———— " The grave, dread thing,
Men shiver when thou'rt named.

*   *   *   *

Well do I know thee by thy trusty yew,
Cheerless, unsocial plant."

THE infinite diversity observable in the works and appearances of nature has already been remarked. In proof of which the sylvan realm offers, perhaps, few stronger contrasts, certainly not in our country, than the light elegant tree we have just been considering, the true similitude of youth and gaiety, and the gloomy, funereal yew, the very sight of which makes us think

———— " Of graves, of worms, and epitaphs,
And choose executors, and talk of wills."

And yet despite its sombre and mournful character, and the opprobrious epithets which poetry has heaped on it, it is a picturesque tree, and one of no inconsiderable

renown. The yew is in high favour with Gilpin. "In a state of nature," says he, "it is, perhaps, one of the most beautiful evergreens we have. Indeed, I know not whether, all things considered, it is not superior to the cedar of Lebanon itself. I mean to such meagre representations of that noble tree as we have in England. The same soil which cramps the cedar is congenial with the yew."

This tree is truly indigenous. When left to its own choice of situation, it grows most freely in mountainous woods, or more particularly in the fissures of limestone rocks; in such places it is still abundant, though far less so than formerly, when "it was to our ancestors what the oak now is to their descendants, the basis of their strength." In those days when we trusted to the bow for our defence, it was ordained by statute that every man should have an English bow, of his own height, made of yew, wych, hazel, ash, or auburn (supposed to be alder). But, "as for brasell, elme, wych, and ash," says Roger Ascham, "experience doth prove them to be mean for bows; and so to conclude, ewe of all other things is that whereof perfite shootinge would have a bowe made." Shakspeare countenances this opinion by the epithet he bestows on it in Richard the Second: —

> " The very beadsmen learn to bend their bows
> Of double fatal yew against thy state."

Such being the mode of warfare, and such the estimation
in which the yew was held for bows, it is no wonder that
the cultivation of it was considered a matter of some
moment; but as the growth of our own country was not
sufficient for the demand, a law was passed by which
merchants were obliged to import a stipulated quantity
of staves for every ton of goods freighted from countries
where the yew was known to grow.

But the fame of this tree for archery does not rest
alone upon the service it rendered to our warlike sires;
we trace it yielding similar aid to nations of high antiquity. Homer thus speaks of it in the hands of the
Cretans:—

> " Cydonians, dreadful with the bended yew."

And Virgil, in the Æneid:—

> " This foul reproach Ascanius could not hear
> With patience, nor a vow'd revenge forbear;
> At the full stretch of both his hands he drew,
> And almost join'd the horns of the tough yew.'

After considering it in this warlike capacity, it is

rather derogatory to see it, as we frequently do, even now, clipped into all sorts of strange and monstrous shapes in the way of adornment. Perhaps no tree has suffered more than this from the treasonable attempts of art to thwart or supplant nature. By our forefathers, who preferred novelty to reality, it was tortured into various forms, as is evident from the relics yet preserved in many old-fashioned gardens. Shenstone playfully condemns this tampering with the wild graces of nature. " Art," says he, " is indeed often requisite to collect and epitomise the beauties of nature, but should never be suffered to set her mark upon them. Why fantastically endeavour to humanise those vegetables of which Nature, discreet Nature, thought it proper to make trees? Why endow the vegetable bird with wings, which Nature has made momentarily dependant upon the soil ? "

The wood of the yew is red, beautifully veined, and very hard and smooth, which makes it valuable for ornamental purposes. Its twigs and leaves are poisonous, and have frequently proved fatal to cattle, and sometimes to the human species. Some extend this pernicious property to the berry; but it is supposed groundlessly, as many persons, ancient and modern, have eaten them without injury. Southey gives countenance to this opinion when, mourning over the fall of some trees, he says,

> " If he had play'd about here when a child
>   In that fore-court, and ate the yew berries,
>   And sate in the porch threading the jessamine flowers
>   Which fell so thick, he had not had the heart
>   To mar them thus."

The leaves, however, as we have already stated, are by common consent deemed poisonous; and it is probably this deadly quality, together with its being usually planted in churchyards, that has led Shakspeare to make " slips of yew" one of the horrible ingredients in his witches' caldron.

The yew is a tree of astonishing longevity; it seems a thing

> " Produced too slowly ever to decay."

So that when we see an aged yew, we may fancy it fraught with the history and legends of centuries.

Like the oak it has obtained much notice from writers on sylvan scenery; and many individuals, celebrated for age, bulk, and legendary renown, are before the public, for the benefit of those who are curious in such subjects.

We must, however, single one from its fellows, not only on account of its great age — for it is said to have flourished upwards of a thousand years, — but for the memorable events with which it is connected. The yew-tree at Ankerwyke, near Staines, " was the silent witness of the conference of those brave barons who afterwards compelled John to sign Magna Charta in its immediate vicinity. It is also said to have been the ill-omened witness of the meetings of the eighth Henry with Anne Boleyn, who was placed at Staines to be near Windsor."

The yew, as has been already observed, delights in mountainous woods and limestone rocks; as, however, in our days, the native stock is greatly diminished, we are most familiar with it as the sentinel of the churchyard, for which habitation its dark evergreen foliage renders it peculiarly appropriate; and we almost merge " the good tough yew" of ancient times, in " the funereal yew" of the present. Yet had it, even in its days of warlike renown, a close connection with the grave, for it has immemorially been the ornament and guardian of country burial places; and what so fit

―――――― " In place of sculptur'd stone,"
To mark " the resting place of men unknown?"

It was also used to deck the corpse, at least so Shakspeare intimates in the following passage:—

> " My shroud of white, stuck all with yew,
>   Oh prepare it ! "

and at the time of interment was carried by the mourners, and afterwards deposited beneath the body, its perpetual verdure being considered a happy emblem of the immortality of the soul.

Few weeks have sped since from yonder pile
    A merry chime was rung,
And blossoms meet for a fair young bride
    On the churchyard path were flung.

But that chime is changed to a doleful knell,
    And those flowers so gay and fair
To funeral wreaths — for the youthful bride
    Now lies shrouded on her bier.

And by white-robed maids is she borne along
    To her grave beneath the shade
Of the lonely yew, and oh ! loud is their wail
    As the last sad rites are paid.

Spell-bound I stood by that sentinel tree,
  And I could not choose but weep,
As one by one that sorrowing train
  Left the dead to her lonely deep.

And as I mused on the fearful sights
  That hoary yew had seen,
'Twas fancy, I know, but methought a voice
  Thus sounded the gusts between: —

' Yes, mortal, yes — I have that to tell
  Would turn Beauty's bright cheek pale,
Would cause the sallies of mirth to cease,
  And e'en warrior's heart to quail.

' I have seen the old, like a shock of corn,
  Safe garner'd in the tomb;
I have seen the babe of a few brief days
  Cut off in its early bloom.

' I have seen the maid, whose cheek was bright
  As a rose in its summer prime,
Droop like that rose 'neath storms or blight,
  And die in youth's budding time.

' I have heard, o'er the grave of her only son,
   The widow her wailings pour;
Then I've seen her turn to her desolate home,
   Now reft both of fence and flower.

' Mortal — thou know'st not how passing short
   Thy number'd days may be,
Oh! then so live that, when comes the last,
   Death may have no sting for thee.'

THE HAZEL.

CORYLUS AVELLANA.

" Season of mists and mellow fruitfulness,
  Close bosom-friend of the maturing sun,
Conspiring with him how to load and bless
  With fruit the vines, that round the thatch'd eaves run ;
To bend with apples the moss'd cottage trees,
  And fill all fruit with ripeness to the core ;
To swell the gourd, and plump the hazel-shells
With a sweet kernel."

THE setting in of autumn is characterised by an increase of splendour in the general aspect of nature.

How clear the cloudless sky ! how deeply ting'd
With a peculiar blue ! the ethereal arch
How swell'd immense ! amid whose azure thron'd,
The radiant sun how gay ! how calm below
  The gilded earth !

At this time the garden assumes a more showy appearance than even summer boasts. The rose and
the lily are followed, in quick succession, by hollyhocks,

dahlias, asters, and other gorgeous flowers, each striving to outvie its neighbour in vividness and variety of colour, not less than in dignity of form and growth.

If we look on the fields,

> " Extensive harvests hang the heavy head,
> A calm of plenty."

Or, in the more emphatic language of Scripture, " The little hills rejoice on every side, the valleys are covered with corn; they shout for joy, they also sing."

If we turn to the woodlands, there is just sufficient diversity in the tints to give beauty and richness to the scene, without reminding us too strongly of decay.

But it is, perhaps, in the orchard that the glory of autumn is most fully displayed.   There,

> ———— " Whate'er the wintry frost
> Nitrous prepar'd, the various-blossom'd spring
> Put in white promise forth, and summer suns
> Concocted strong, rush boundless now to view,
> Full, perfect all."

In lands of " the sweet south," the olive, the fig, the orange, and, above all, the vine, are seen mingling their rich and varied fruitage.   In our less genial climate, besides those fruits which require artificial heat, we can show plums of various kinds, pears, apples, filberts; and not only in the orchard, but in every coppice, and haunting every stream, the hazel, so eulogized by the poet, so dear to our childhood.

Burns leads us adown many a hazelly path, where "twin nuts cluster thick;" and we almost hear

> " The little birdies blythely sing,
> While o'er their heads the hazels hing,
> Or lightly flit on wanton wing,
> In the birks of Aberfeldy."

Virgil makes frequent mention of "the tangling hazel." Indeed, in the following passage, he gives it more honour than is due: —

> " Alcides' brows the poplar leaves surround,
> Apollo's beamy locks with bays are crown'd,
> The myrtle, lovely queen of smiles, is thine,
> And jolly Bacchus loves the curling vine;
> But while my Phyllis loves the hazel-spray,
> To hazel yield the myrtle and the bay."

In his second Georgic, however, he is less complimentary to our favourite, positively forbidding, on account of some supposed noxious quality, its entrance into the vineyard: —

> " The hurtful hazel in the vineyard shun."

Shakspeare, in the "Taming of the Shrew," says, —

" Kate, like the hazel twig, is straight and slender; and brown in hue
as hazel nuts, and sweeter than the kernels."

And Thomson, whom no rural sound or sight escapes,
describing the various haunts which different birds
select for their nests, mentions some as choosing

> —— " shaggy banks
> Steep and divided by a babbling brook,
> Whose murmurs soothe them all the livelong day
> When by kind duty fix'd   Among the roots
> Of hazel, pendent o'er the plaintive stream,
> They form the first foundation of their domes."

These are but a few of the poetical notices of this
rural favourite; but it has other and dearer claims on
our regard than those which arise from its classical
fame. "When we think of the lovely scenes into
which the careless steps of our youth have been led,"
says a writer we have frequently quoted, "in search
of its nuts, when autumn had begun to brown the
points of their clusters, we are bound to it by threads
of the most delightful associations with those beloved

ones who were the companions of such idle but happy days." How well can the heart respond to these reminiscences! for a proneness to dwell with pleasure on the sports of our early years, and to retrace those scenes

> " Where erst our careless childhood stray'd,
>   A stranger yet to pain,"

is a universal passion; and among those sports nutting has ever held the foremost place. What a lively picture Thomson gives us of this rural pastime; and how feelingly, too, Wordsworth describes it, though, in this instance, his was a solitary joy: —

> —— " It seems a day
> (I speak of one from many singled out),
> One of those heavenly days which cannot die;
> When, in the eagerness of boyish hope,
> I left our cottage threshold, sallying forth,
> With a huge wallet o'er my shoulder slung,
> A nutting, crook in hand, and turn'd my steps
> Towards the distant woods, — a figure quaint,
> Trick'd out in proud disguise of cast-off weeds
> Which for that service had been husbanded,
> Motley accoutrement, of power to smile
> At thorns and brakes and brambles, and in truth
> More rugged than need was. Among the woods,
> And o'er the pathless rocks I forced my way,

Until at length I came to one dear nook
Unvisited, where not a broken bough
Droop'd with its wither'd leaves, ungracious sign
Of devastation; but the hazels rose
Tall and erect, with milk-white clusters hung —
A virgin scene! A little while I stood,
Breathing with such suppression of the heart
As joy delights in; and with wise restraint
Voluptuous, fearless of a rival, eyed
The banquet — or beneath the trees I sate
Among the flowers, and with the flowers I play'd.

——— " Then up I rose,
And dragg'd to earth both branch and bough, with crash
And merciless ravage; and the shady nook
Of hazels, and the green and mossy bower,
Deform'd and sullied, patiently gave up
Their quiet being."

The hazel grows wild in almost every part of Great Britain, but it most prefers a sandy soil, and cold mountainous situations; indeed, it ranks amongst those hardy trees which are found in very high latitudes.

There are only two species of corylus, — our hazel, of which the filbert is merely a variety; and corylus colurna, the Byzantine nut. " The hazel," says Swinburn, " has the name Avellana from Avellino, a city of the kingdom of Naples, where it is much cultivated, and covers the whole face of the neighbouring valley, and in good years brings in a profit of sixty thousand ducats. The nuts are mostly of the large round filbert, which we call Spanish. They were originally brought into Italy from Pontus, and known amongst the Romans by the appellation of nux Pontica, which, in process of time, was changed into that of nux Avellana, from the place where they had been propagated with the greatest success."

The origin of the euphonious title of Caledonia, by which that tasteful people distinguished Scotland, arose, according to Sir William Temple, from the following circumstance: — " The north-west part was called Cal-Dun, signifying hills of hazel, with which it was covered; from which the Romans, forming an easy and pleasant sound out of what was harsh to their classical ear, gave it the name of Caledonia."

The hazel is amongst our earliest flowering trees; in mild seasons, its beautiful pendulous catkins show themselves even in January. It is amongst trees what the snowdrop is amongst flowers, the first herald of spring.

To sum up briefly its claims on our regard: it cheers us with its bloom ere " the winter is over and gone;" in autumn it yields us "fruit, pleasant to the eyes, and

good for food;" it furnishes us with many poetical associations; it offers recreation to the young; and, more
than all, in later years, the sight of it sends such a re
newal of youthful feeling into the heart, that, for a while
at least, the present, with its perplexities and sorrows, is
merged in the past, when our cares were " as the morning cloud," and our tears " as the early dew that passeth
away."

Ere yet pale Autumn on the leaf-strew'd ground
   Sits like a widow, sad and desolate,
Weeping, with mantle rent and head discrown'd,
   The vanish'd glory of her early state,
She hath an hour of triumph and of pride,
When, bless'd and blessing, through earth's circuit wide
She walks with laughing Plenty at her side.
She looks around with warm, maturing smile,
And waving harvests ask the reaper's toil;
She gives the vine (child of a southern sky)
Its pulpy nectar, and its Tyrian dye;
She ripens the green germ which Summer won
From Spring's empurpled blossoms, — and anon

The orchard's mossy boughs, with fruitage crown'd,
Stoop with their mellow burden to the ground;
While in the tangled copse of tawny hue,
The clustering hazel tempts the wanderer's view.
The clustering hazel! — ah! as with a spell
Those few brief words recall the bygone hours,
When the heart's pulse was music, and on flowers, —
Bright, thornless flowers, my footsteps ever fell.
Ev'n now, methinks, I see the bushy dell,
The tangled brake, green lane, or sunny glade,
Where " on a sunshine holiday," I strayed,
Plucking the ripening nuts with eager glee,
Which from the hazel boughs hung temptingly;
Till falling dews, and floweret's closing bell,
To my unwilling heart did Eve's dim reign foretell.

'T is not, O Time! that thou dost pale the rose
On youth's fair cheek, or stain the lily's snows;
(Mar as thou wilt these graces of our prime) —
'T is not for this I dread thee, ruthless Time!
'T is that thou tam'st the spirits, check'st the play
Of youthful fancy, turn'st our matin lay
To dirge-like music, changest hopes to fears,
And for one smile call'st forth uncounted tears.

Season of bliss! return, return once more,
When, yet untaught in sorrow's darkling lore,
The heart, all sunshine, with its own sweet light
Tinges whate'er arrests the wondering sight,
O'er Spring's blue skies a brighter lustre throws,
And gives a livelier tint to Summer's rose.
Take, keep, what else thou wilt, so thou restore
O, changing Time! this *youth of heart* once more!

THE FIG.

FICUS CARICA.

" Close to the gates a spacious garden lies,
From storms defended and inclement skies ;
Here the blue fig with luscious juice o'erflows,
With deeper red the full pomegranate glows ;
Here order'd vines in equal ranks appear,
And verdant olives flourish all the year.
The balmy spirit of the western gale
Eternal breathes on fruits untaught to fail ;
Each dropping pear a following pear supplies,
On apples, apples, figs on figs arise :
The same mild season gives the blooms to blow,
The buds to harden, and the fruits to grow."

" GOD ALMIGHTY first planted a garden," says Lord Bacon : " it is the purest of human pleasures ; it is the greatest refreshment to the spirits of man." And in so saying he does not speak unadvisedly, or from envy or ignorance, for he had tasted, and that not sparingly, all the pleasures which station, wealth, and learning can bestow ; but, in despite of them all, he thus gives it

as his opinion that the simplest pleasures are the best.
In the above description of the garden of Alcinous, we
have all that riches and taste can heap together; but it
does not require "this gay profusion of luxurious bliss"
to make a garden the source both of healthful employ-
ment and sincere gratification. "Happy they that can
create a rose-tree, or erect a honeysuckle," says the poet
Gray; "that can watch the brood of a hen, or see a fleet
of their own ducklings launch into the water."

In most parts of Italy the fig, the vine, and the olive
abound.

What a beautifully vivid picture the poet, lately
quoted, gives of the route towards Naples! "The
minute one leaves his Holiness' dominions, the face of
things begins to change from wide uncultivated plains
to olive groves and well-tilled fields of corn, intermixed
with rows of elms, every one of which has its vine twining about it, and hanging in festoons between the rows
from one tree to another. The great old fig-trees, the
oranges in full bloom, and myrtles in every hedge,
make one of the most delightful scenes you can conceive."

Dissimilar as are these trees, both in their mode
of growth and their produce, they are yet constantly
associated in the imagination. The reason of this is,

not only because they are so frequently seen grouped together in eastern and southern landscapes (the same soil and temperature being common to each), but because they are always mentioned conjunctively in the Scriptures as symbols and proofs of prosperity and fertility. "The Lord thy God bringeth thee into a good land; * * * a land of vines, and fig-trees, and pomegranates; a land of oil, olive, and honey." Deut. viii. 8. And when Joshua sent men to see the promised land, and bring a report of it and specimens of the fruits, " they came unto the brook Eschol, and cut down from thence a branch with one cluster of grapes, and they bare it between two upon a staff: and they brought of the pomegranates and of the figs."

But we must leave the vine and the olive for future consideration, and direct our attention wholly to the fig. It is confessedly a native of Asia, but whether of any parts of Europe is a matter of conjecture; if not really indigenous, however, it has been cultivated there from the most remote antiquity. It is mentioned by Homer, not only in the lines selected for the motto, but also as surmounting a rock near where " Charybdis holds her boisterous reign."

> " Full on its crown a fig's green branches rise,
> And shoot a leafy forest to the skies."

And in another passage he says, —

"There figs, sky-dyed, a purple hue disclose."

It was dedicated by the Romans to Saturn as the patron of agriculture; they crowned his statue with its fruit; they planted it at the entrance to his temple; and also bore it in procession next in order to the vine in their bacchanalian festivals. The fig was held in the highest estimation, in early times, for its nutritious qualities; and formed then, as now, a grateful repast to people whose primitive taste requires little else than fruits, vegetables, bread, and water. It was one of the articles of food allowed at the common tables established by Lycurgus; and by the Athenians it was deemed of so much importance, in this point of view, that their exportation was strictly prohibited. A failure in the crop was considered by the Jews a national calamity; and when judgment was denounced against their land, this was always part of the curse, "There shall be no grapes on the vines, nor figs on the fig-tree."

Though this tree never attains any very considerable height, yet its broad mantling foliage forms a delightful shelter from the ardent rays of the sun in those burning climes. This is often beautifully alluded to in holy writ; as in Micah, "And they shall sit every man under his vine, and under his fig-tree, and none shall make them afraid."

It is gratefully mentioned by most modern travellers. Burckhardt recalls with enthusiasm the refreshing shade it afforded him in the neighbourhood of Tiberias, when overcome by the intense heat of a mid-day sun. Haselquist also bears the same testimony. We shall quote his words, as they form quite a pastoral landscape truly eastern: — " We refreshed ourselves beneath a fig-tree, under which was a well, where a shepherd and his flock had their rendezvous; but without either house or hut."

Respecting the date of the introduction of the fig into Britain, authors hold different opinions: some think it was brought hither by our Roman conquerors; others place it several centuries later, and state that Cardinal Pole planted the first specimens in the palace garden at Lambeth. These identical trees are still in being, and till very lately were in a most flourishing condition, covering a space of fifty feet in height and forty in breadth, and bearing delicious fruit.

This fruit, however, appears never to have been congenial with the English taste; for, though it takes more kindly to our climate than either the vine or the olive, certainly than the latter, its cultivation has always been very limited; the common proverb, too, which is in use, when any thing is spoken of disparagingly, corroborates this opinion. Shakspeare makes frequent mention of it in this sense. Among later poets, Thomson names it in his beautiful description of autumnal fruits: —

> " Here, as I steal along the sunny wall,
> Where Autumn basks, with fruits empurpled deep,
> My pleasing theme continual prompts my thought;
> Presents the downy peach; the shining plum;
> The ruddy, fragrant nectarine; and, dark
> Beneath its ample leaf, the luscious fig."

There are many species of the genus ficus, amongst which are the sycamore fig, so frequently mentioned in scripture, and the celebrated banian or Indian fig.

The fig sometimes bears a triple crop, thus supplying the inhabitants of the countries where it grows with fruit a great part of the year. The first ripe figs, according to Dr. Shaw, "are called boccôre, and come to maturity about the latter end of June, though, like other fruit, they yield a few ripe before the full season." These are probably of inferior value *; for the prophet Hosea says, " I found Israel like grapes in the wilderness; I saw

---

* This seems a little at variance with a passage in Jeremiah, xxiv. 2. " One basket had very good figs, even *like the figs that are first ripe*."

your fathers as the first ripe in the fig-tree at her first time." When the boccôre draws near perfection, the karmouse, or summer fig, begins to be formed. This is the crop which is dried. When the karmouse ripens, in Syria and Barbary, there appears a third crop, which often hangs and ripens upon the tree after the leaves are shed."

This tree is frequently alluded to in the New Testament. The curse denounced against the barren fig-tree is too striking an event to be passed unnoticed. In reference to it, Hartwell Horne, in his Introduction to the Critical Study of the Scriptures, has the following remark : — "It is a well-known fact that the fruit of these prolific trees always precedes the leaves; consequently, when Jesus Christ saw one of them in full vigour *having leaves,* he might, according to the common course of nature, very justly *look for fruit,* and haply find some boccôres or early figs, if not some winter figs upon it."

Besides the immediate inference which our blessed Saviour himself pointed out to his wondering disciples from this circumstance, namely, the power of faith, it seems capable of affording another lesson. Does it not intimate the danger of a false and fruitless profession? "Every branch," says our Lord, "in me that beareth not fruit, he taketh away."

Short time ago, and yonder tree
Waved in the light breeze gloriously;
And to the morning sun displayed
Proudly its amplitude of shade.

Say, then, what storm, what sudden blast,
With poison'd breath, has o'er it pass'd,
That thus like shrivell'd scroll it shows
With wither'd leaves and drooping boughs?

Each flower sleeps peaceful on its stem,
Each spray the pendent dew-drops gem;
How then could sudden blast or storm
Have ravaged thus its stately form?

It was His word who spake at first
Creation into life: — He curs'd
That fated tree — the spell of power
It own'd, and wither'd in an hour.

And what provoked the doom severe?
Its trunk was firm, its boughs were fair;
Its leaves in gold and emerald shone:
He sought for fruit—but fruit was none.

Ah! who so blind as not to read
A fearful meaning in the deed?
On me, on all, a searching eye
Is bent in awful scrutiny.

What if within these hearts of ours,
For fruit, it sees but leaves or flowers?
Ah! who may tell how long the doom
Shall threaten ere its thunders come!

Awhile, at Mercy's earnest suit,
The voice of Justice may be mute;
But never will she sheathe her sword,
While man—the worm—defies the Lord!

Oh! strong to punish, strong to save!
How long shall we Thy fury brave?
How long?—till Thou thyself embue
Each callous heart with heavenly dew.

Hast Thou not said, in wilds forlorn
The myrtle shall supplant the thorn?
Fulfil Thy promise, then shall we
Yield fruits of holiness to Thee!

THE VINE.

VITIS VINIFERA.

" Turn we a moment Fancy's rapid flight
  To vigorous soils, and climes of fair extent,
  Where, by the potent sun elated high,
  The vineyard swells refulgent on the day;
  Spreads o'er the vale, or up the mountain climbs
  Profuse; and drinks amid the sunny rocks,
  From cliff to cliff increased, the heighten'd blaze.
  Low bend the weighty boughs; the clusters clear
  Half through the foliage seen, or ardent flame,
  Or shine transparent, while perfection breathes
  White o'er the turgent film the living dew."

BEAUTIFUL and glowing as is this description of the
vine, we may yet truly say it needs not the poet's pencil
to enhance its charms; for when left to follow its own
elegant fancies, and to twine its tendrils to any prop
which offers itself, it does indeed

" Outstrip all praise,
And make it halt behind."

Such is its character, in many parts of Spain and Italy, where it is not cultivated for wine. It is then seen with the most picturesque effect, hanging its gay festoons to neighbouring trees, asking support, and giving beauty. Southey has the following beautiful description of it: —

> " These scenes profusely blest by Heaven they left,
> Where o'er the hazel and the quince, the vine
> Wide mantling spreads ; and, clinging round the cork
> And ilex, hangs amid their dusky leaves
> Garlands of brightest hue, with reddening fruit
> Pendent, or clusters cool of glassy green. "

In those parts, however, where it is cultivated for wine, all its native gracefulness is lost; and in France and Germany especially, "the pole-clipt vineyards," as Shakspeare rightly designates them, are always disappointing objects to travellers who are unprepared for their appearance under culture. The vines are trained to poles, seldom more than a yard high, and all their wild luxuriance is pruned, the more to enhance the size and flavour of the fruit. In the latter country they are constantly seen mingling their trellised branches, laden with translucent clusters, the very image of plenty, with the ruined fortresses and baronial castles which overhang the Rhine; and there, though still suffering from the pruning knife, they look

well from contrast — most assuredly they do so in
poetry : —

> " Above the frequent feudal towers,
>   Through green leaves lift their walls of gray,
>   And many a rock which steeply lours,
>   And noble arch in proud decay,
>   Look o'er this vale of vintage bowers "

The earliest *authentic* history we have of the cultivation of this tree is in the book of Genesis, where we
are told, " Noah began to be a husbandman, and he
planted a vineyard." If, however, we might trust to
poetry, we should find that it was of yet prior date; for
it is described as one of the pleasant pursuits of our
first parents to lead

> —— " The vine
> To wed her elm."

We also learn from the same authority, that in that
garden of bliss, there were

> —— " Umbrageous grots, and caves
> Of cool recess, o'er which the mantling vine
> Laid forth her purple grape, and gently crept
> Luxuriant."

The next *poetical* intimation we have of its culture is from Homer : —

> " Here order'd vines in equal ranks appear,
> With all th' united labours of the year;
> Some to unload the fertile branches run,
> Some dry the blackening clusters in the sun,
> Others to tread the liquid harvest join, —
> The groaning presses foam with floods of wine ;
> Here are the vines in early flower descried,
> Here grapes discolour'd on the sunny side,
> And there in Autumn's richest purple dyed. "

Fiction, however, apart, the cultivation of the vine was certainly a matter of great moment in the East. The vineyards were most commonly planted on the southern side of a hill, and surrounded by walls, or a hedge of thorns, every thing being first cleared away which might injure the growth of the plants ; a striking commentary this on the first and second verses in the fifth chapter of Isaiah. Palestine abounded in vines, particularly in the district allotted to Judah ; in which were contained Eschol and Engeddi, so famous for their vineyards. Thus was the prediction of the patriarch fulfilled : — " Binding his foal unto the vine, and his ass's colt unto the choice vine: he washed his garments in wine, and his clothes in the blood of the grape."

As a symbol of joy and plenty, the vine is perpetually recurring in Scripture. Besides the prophecy just quoted, we find when Isaac invoked a blessing on Jacob he said, " God give thee of the dew of heaven, and the fatness of the earth, and plenty of corn and wine."

Such are a few of the passages where it is referred to in the Old Testament: in the Gospels it is connected with more touching associations. With solemnised feelings, we remember who hath said, " I am the vine, ye are the branches; he that abideth in me, and I in him, the same bringeth forth much fruit." And with yet deeper emotion we recall to mind the sacramental supper, and who it was that " took the cup and blessed it, saying, Drink ye all of it; for this is my blood of the New Testament, which is shed for many for the remission of sins."

Like most other choice fruits, the vine migrated from the East to the West. Some writers affirm it is truly wild in Greece, a circumstance which others doubt; but if not indigenous, from a very remote period it has been completely naturalised both there and in other parts of southern Europe, where its culture has long formed a chief branch of rural economy.

Virgil, who seems almost as good a naturalist as a poet, discourses very learnedly on the cultivation both of the vine and olive, in his second Georgic. He informs us how, and when, and where to plant these valuable trees, in strains so sweet that the rough labours of husbandry appear no longer a part of the original curse. Speaking of the natural habitat of the vine, he says, —

> " Nor every plant on every soil will grow :
> The sallow loves the wat'ry ground, and low ;
> The marshes alders. Nature seems t' ordain
> The rocky cliffs for the wild ash's reign ;
> The baleful yew to northern blasts assigns,
> To shores the myrtles, and to mounts the vines."

But when under culture, he allows the situation to be a matter of choice, recommending only a corresponding difference in the mode of planting : —

> " Choose next a province for thy vineyard's reign
> On hills above, or in the lowly plain :
> If fertile fields or valleys be thy choice,
> Plant *thick*, for bounteous Bacchus will rejoice
> In *close* plantations *there*. But if the vine
> On rising ground be placed, or hills supine,
> Extend thy loose battalions largely wide,
> Opening thy ranks and files on either side ;
> But marshall'd all in order as they stand,
> And let no soldier straggle from his band."

The softness of the Italian climate, and the luxuriance of the vineyards, are supposed to have been the lure which tempted the northern hordes to ravage that fair land, whose curse has ever been " the fatal gift of beauty." How fine is the poet's description ! —

> " The prostrate South to the destroyer yields
> Her boasted titles and her golden fields :
> With grim delight the brood of winter view
> A brighter day, and heavens of azure hue,
> Scent the new fragrance of the breathing rose,
> And quaff the pendent vintage as it grows."

The vine appears to be more fastidious with regard to temperature than to soil : it is almost equally adverse to extremes of heat and cold, and is only cultivated with advantage from the 21° to 51° of northern latitude; but with respect to the latter, though it prefers such as is light and gravelly, it will grow almost on any soil ; nay, we are told by the poet that

> " *Leanest* land supplies the richest wine."

It is a tree of amazing longevity, even superior to that of the oak itself, and is in a condition to bear fruit many hundred years. Its wood is very durable, and its stem sometimes attains a considerable bulk. The great doors of the cathedral of Ravenna are made of vine planks.

Of the first introduction of this beautiful and valuable tree amongst us, there are no authentic records; but it is generally supposed we are indebted for it to the Romans, towards the close of the time that they held our island in subjection.

It was certainly cultivated here under the Saxon dynasty, as vineyards are mentioned in the earliest Saxon charters. Winchester, and many other places, are supposed to have derived their name from the extensive vineries in their immediate neighbourhood. The Vale of Gloucester was famous for its vines; and in the days of popery every monastery had its vineyard, for the foreign monks inherited from their own more genial climes a predilection for the juice of the grape. And still in some of our southern counties,

> ———— " The vine her curling tendrils shoots,
> Hangs out her clusters glowing to the south,
> And scarcely wishes for a warmer sky."

Generally speaking, however, we find its culture disregarded, except as an article of luxury in our stoves, or blended with woodbine and other climbing plants as

an ornament to our houses and cottages. Milton gives
us a beautiful sketch of it in this position : —

> " To hear the lark begin his flight,
> And singing startle the dull night,
> From his watch-tower in the skies,
> Till the dappled morn arise :
> Then to come in spite of sorrow,
> And at my window bid good-morrow
> Through the sweet-brier, or the vine,
> Or the twisted eglantine."

No plant, perhaps, has so much classical fame as the
vine. It has been the favourite theme of poetry in all
ages and in all countries. We select the following from
Homer's multitudinous store : —

> " Depending vines the shelving caverns screen,
> With purple clusters blushing through the green."

And from Virgil : —

> " For now the year in brightest glory shines,
> Now reddening clusters deck the bending vines."

Among our own poets, Shakspeare, in Henry the Fifth,
speaking of the effects of protracted war in France,
says, —

——— " Her husbandry doth lie in heaps,
Corrupting in its own fertility ,
Her vine, the merry cheerer of the heart,
Unpruned dies "

In Henry the Eighth he borrows prophetic imagery, and applies it to the security and prosperity predicted by the prelate under Elizabeth's sway : —

" In her days every man shall eat in safety,
Under his own vine, what he plants ; and sing
The merry songs of peace to all his neighbours "

In Comus, when the disguised enchanter gives information to the lady of her belated brothers, he says, —

" I saw them under a green mantling vine,
That crawls along the side of yon small hill,
Plucking ripe clusters from the tender shoots ;
Their port was more than human as they stood.
I took it for a faëry vision
Of some gay creatures of the elements,
That in the colours of the rainbow live,
And play i' th' plighted clouds."

The whole description is so very beautiful, we could not forbear quoting it.

In his fine poem of the " Messiah," Pope thus describes the blessings of His reign : —

" Their vines a shadow to their race shall yield,
And the same hand that sow'd shall reap the field."

One more sketch from the pen of a modern poet,
which admirably comprises, in one glowing view, the
various features of a southern landscape : —

" The horrid crags by toppling convent crown'd,
The cork-trees hoar that clothe the shaggy steep,
The mountain moss by scorching skies embrown'd,
The sunken glen whose sunless herbs must weep,
The tender azure of th' unruffled deep,
The orange tints that gild the greenest bough,
The torrents that from cliff to valley leap,
The vine on high, the willow branch below,
Mix'd in one mighty scene with varied beauty glow."

The magnificent clusters of beautiful fruit which adorn
its branches are the produce of a remarkably small
insignificant flower, which possesses, however, in a considerable degree, the redeeming quality of fragrance;
a quality for which Lord Bacon greatly commends it.
" Next to the violet," says he, " is the musk rose; then
the strawberry leaves dying, with a most excellent cor-
dial smell; then the flower of the vine, — it is a little
dust, like the dust of a bent, which grows upon the
cluster in the first coming forth."   But we can adduce

far higher authority than his in praise of the perfume of
this little flower: he who "spake of trees, from the cedar
tree that is in Lebanon, even unto the hyssop that
springeth out of the wall," says, "The fig-tree putteth
forth her green figs, and the vines with the tende
grapes give a good smell."

THE VINE IN FLOWER.

'Is this thy whole of bloom?   Does Spring
  No richer, brighter garland fling
    Around thy stem?
Then surely it is but in sport
That thou dost ask in Flora's court
    A place and name.'

'Ah! spare thy taunt; I know full well
  In me no floral beauties dwell:
    The meanest weed
That blossoms in the public way,
In grace of form, in colours gay,
    Doth me exceed.

'But come when Autumn's genial hour
  Has changed to fruit my puny flower,
    And from my bough
The purple nectar freely sip;
And whilst it cools thy parched lip
    And fever'd brow,

' Oh ! learn with more discerning eyes,
  Whate'er its aspect or disguise,
     True worth to scan ;
  And, better taught, in time to come,
  Pause ere thou hastily fore-doom
     Thy fellow-man.'

IN FRUIT.

And such is then thy Autumn dower !
Such clusters from so mean a flower !
   How can it be ?
If Flora slight thee, yet I trow
Pomona's pride and boast art thou,
   Thou glorious tree !

Thou, to whom bards of old did string
The viol, and thy praises sing
   In various lay, —
I, too, though feeble be my lyre,
To laud thy beauty would aspire,
   But not as they.

Their loudest pæans were outpour'd
When freely at the festal board
 Thy nectar flow'd;
When in the cup it mov'd aright,
And to the eye like ruby bright
 Its colour show'd.

Whilst I — I love thee best, fair vine,
When thou from tree to tree dost twine
 Thy fruitful boughs;
When pleasant both to sight and taste,
With more than fabled beauty grac'd,
 Each cluster glows.

If glad of heart, I'll sit and dream
Of vintage time, and to the theme
 With cadence true
I'll wake to blithsome strains my lute,
Blithsome yet pure — as on thy fruit
 " The living dew." .

If grave — oh! is't not thine to take
A more than moral tone, and wake
 Sweet Sabbath moods,

By minding us of what thou art
The type — till lighter thoughts depart,
And on divinest themes the heart
　　In quiet broods.

THE OLIVE.

OLEA.

" And he stayed yet other seven days: and again he sent forth the dove out of the ark.

" And the dove came in to him in the evening; and, lo, in her mouth was an olive leaf plucked off: so Noah knew that the waters were abated from off the earth."

SUCH is our first introduction to the olive; which seems to be on earth what the bow is in the sky, — the harbinger and the token of peace.

Whether from the event which the sacred text records is not certain, but its pacific character has been acknowledged in all times, and among all nations; it is, however, more than probable that it owes its celebrity in this point of view to traditionary lore, for many ancient customs and notions among the heathen have so close an affinity to transactions related in the Bible, that, however changed and blended with fable, it is almost beyond conjecture that they were originally derived from that sacred source.

In this character, as the symbol of peace, it is noticed by innumerable authors, ancient and modern.

> " High on the stern Eneas took his stand,
> And held a branch of olive in his hand."

And again, —

> " Now suppliants from Laurentum sent demand
> A truce, with olive branches in their hand."

So sings Virgil.

In the pages of our own poets it figures largely.
Spenser mentions it thus : —

> " His right hand did the peaceful olive wield."

And Shakspeare in many passages; a few of which
must suffice. The following is from Antony and Cleo-
patra : —

> " The time of universal peace is near :
> Prove this a prosperous day, the three-nooked world
> Shall bear the olive freely."

In Timon of Athens —

> ———— " Bring me into your city,
> And I will use the olive with my sword :
> Make war breed peace, make peace stint war."

And in the Twelfth Night, Viola, in declaring her mis-
sion to Olivia, says, —

"I bring no overture of war, no taxation of homage; I hold the olive in my hand: my words are as full of peace as matter."

Milton associates it with holier recollections, and brings us back to the Flood.

> "Forthwith from out the ark a raven flies,
> And after him the surer messenger,
> A dove, sent forth once and again to spy
> Green tree or ground whereon his foot may light:
> The second time returning in his bill
> An olive-leaf he brings, pacific sign."

He introduces it again, most beautifully, in his Ode on the Nativity: —

> "But he her fears to cease,
> Sent down the meek-eyed Peace,
>   She, crown'd with olive-green, came softly gliding
> Down through the turning sphere,
> His ready harbinger
>   With turtle wings the amorous clouds dividing."

Unnumbered poetical allusions to the olive, of great beauty, ancient and modern, present themselves, which, for the sake of brevity, we pass by, selecting only from the mass the following expressive lines from Prior: —

> "The winds fall silent, and the waves decrease,
> The dove brings quiet, and the olive peace."

The olive, as we have already stated, was held in the highest esteem in Judea, and was there not only regarded as the emblem of peace, but also of plenty. Under the Mosaic dispensation it was consecrated to the most solemn uses. Its oil fed the lamps of the sanctuary; of its wood Solomon made the doors of the oracle, and also the two cherubim contained within. At the feast of tabernacles, olive branches, blended with pine, myrtle, willow, and palm, were borne in procession and formed into booths, according to divine command.

The olive is also employed largely in prophetic imagery, to denote the future peace and prosperity of the church of God. " I will plant in the wilderness, the cedar, the shittah tree, and the myrtle, and the oil (or olive) tree."

But, like the vine, the most thrilling associations are those which it derives from the events with which it stands connected in the New Testament. What scene so sacred, so endearing to the Christian, as " the Mount of Olives !" There the Redeemer of the world frequently repaired; there he predicted the destruction of Jerusalem; on his descent from it " he beheld the city, and wept over it; " and at its foot was the garden of Gethsemane — that hallowed spot which witnessed

"The grief which angels cannot tell,—
Our God in agony !"

Such are the recollections this tree awakens; recollections which connect it—how closely! how touchingly!—with the moral history of man. It bore tidings to the patriarch of the assuaging waters, — to the Christian it speaks of a second deliverance, through Him who " in his love and in his pity redeemed him."

As if to bear testimony to its former fertility, the olive still grows plentifully in Judea, and also in Syria. From these lands it is supposed originally to have been transported to southern Europe. Pliny, who gives the preference to the olive above all other fruit-bearing trees, except the vine, says, that "Italy and Africa were both strangers to it two centuries after the building of Rome; after being well naturalised in which countries, it was carried thence into Spain and Gaul."

In Greece it was cultivated at a very early period; particularly in the neighbourhood of Athens, in which place it was held in the greatest veneration. Superstition had its share in the esteem with which the inhabitants regarded it; for they believed it to be the special boon of Minerva herself to their favoured city, on which account they chose her for their tutelary deity, and paid her divine honours. The legend of the olive and the horse, the respective gifts of Minerva and Neptune, is familiar to every reader.

The ancients supposed the olive to be a maritime tree; but though it does thrive better near the sea than most others, it will flourish remarkably well at a distance from that element, provided the temperature be mild and balmy; for, like its companion, the vine, it is more affected by temperature than soil. It certainly prefers calcareous soil, but will grow on any kind. This difference, however, marks its growth, according to the ground in which it is planted: in such as is rich and moist, it becomes a larger, handsomer tree; whilst in poor and meagre land, it produces the best fruit. This fact seems to illustrate the passage in Deut. xxxii. 13. — " He made him to suck honey out of the rock, and oil out of the flinty rock."

It is a tree of tardy growth. To this Virgil alludes, when he speaks of

" The slow product of Minerva's tree."

He also adverts to another property it possesses, — its power of resuscitation : —

" E'en stumps of olives, bar'd of leaves and dead,
Revive, and oft redeem their wither'd head."

Its wood, which is of a reddish tint, is hard and close-grained, and takes a fine polish; on which account it was much prized by the ancients, both for ornamental and useful works. We are told by Homer that the handle of the axe given by Calypso to Ulysses was

> —————— " Smooth and plain,
> Wrought of the clouded olive's easy grain."

The olive is cultivated to a great extent in Italy, Spain, and the south of France, for the sake of the oil produced from its berries. Gray speaks of it as growing profusely in Lombardy. The olive is altogether too tender to flourish well in our ungenial climate. In the mildest winters it requires shelter; and only under very favourable circumstances will it produce fruit, which is flavourless, and never ripens. It also changes its character; and instead of retaining its leaves through the winter, as it does in those " lands of the sun," it sheds them like the deciduous trees. But, though we cannot boast of

> —————— " Fruitful vines and the fat olive's freight,
> Yet harvests heavy with their fruitful weight
> Adorn our fields."

And whilst corn, the staff of life, is ours, we may well be content to borrow wine and oil from our neighbours.

Its mode of growth is peculiar. Several stems rise from the same root to the height of from twenty to thirty feet, covered with a grey bark. It bears a delicate white flower, in some species very fragrant; and its leaves are of a lively green on the upper surface, but hoary underneath.

It is, individually, a beautiful and graceful object; but when cultivated largely, as in the olive countries, for purposes of commerce, it adds no charm to the landscape. An olive ground has a dull and cold tone of colouring, something the same in effect as a grove of willows, which we know would require the relief of brighter-hued trees.

But if such be the appearance of this tree in nature, under the alchymical touch of poetry it looks all that the untravelled have ever imagined it. How beautifully is it introduced into this Spanish landscape! —

> —————— " In such an hour
> The vesper melody of dying bells
> Wanders through Spain from each grey convent's tower,
> O'er shining rivers pour'd, and olive dells."

Here is another picture by the same gifted pencil, and from the same bright realm: —

" Here the eye roves through slender colonnades,
O'er bowery terraces and myrtle shades ;
Dark olive woods beyond, and far on high
The vast sierra, mingling with the sky."

These are Spanish scenes ; but now the muse leads us to another land, where we still keep the olive in view ; for lo ! —

———— " Arno wins us to the fair white walls,
Where the Etrurian Athens claims and keeps
A softer feeling for her fairy halls.
Girt by her theatre of hills, she reaps
Her corn, and wine, and oil, and Plenty leaps
To laughing life with her redundant horn."

" In such a world, — so thorny," so full of jarring interests and conflicting passions, how sweet is any thing which breathes of peace ! It is for this we love the olive. " They who rejoice when their corn, and their wine, and their oil are increased," will delight in it as the symbol of plenty; but the meek and gentle-hearted, the wounded in spirit, will love it best as the harbinger of peace.

I would not, if I might,
Child of my heart! the hidden page unseal,
That would thy future destiny reveal.
How should I shrink aghast
To see fierce passions glass'd
On that fair brow, which feels as yet no blight!
Enough to know that often thou must stray,
With sackcloth round thee spread,
And ashes on thy head,
A weeping pilgrim on life's weary way.

Oh! rather let me pray, when bursts the cloud —
When deep to deep is calling long and loud,
That He, the heavenly Dove,
With healing wing would move
Upon these troubled waters of the soul,
Hushing their turbulence with sweet control;
And when the storm has work'd His will who gave
Strength to the wind and fury to the wave,
He, like the bird which told the flood's decrease,
Would yield to thee at last like pledge of love and peace.

Oh! were it mine to choose from earthly bower
Aught that might shape, with talismanic power,

Thy future path, not Beauty's type — the rose —
Should tempt my hand, because 'mid thorns it grows;
  Nor myrtle's lovelorn spray,
  Nor ivy-wreath, nor bay,
  Should thy fair brow entwine,
  Or in thy bosom shine.
  All, all which they proclaim, —
  Mirth, beauty, pleasure, fame, —
Child of my heart!　I gladly would resign,
If but that richer boon — sweet peace — be thine.
What would I more?　If but to thee be given
The olive-bough on earth, — the conqueror's palm in
   heaven!

THE BAY AND PALM.

THE BAY.

LAURUS NOBILIS.

"The laurel, meed of mighty conquerors
And poets sage."

THE Laurus Nobilis, or sweet bay, though but a shrub in our country, in Asia and the southern parts of Europe, its proper birthplace, attains to the height of twenty or thirty feet. It grows very freely on the banks of the river Peneus in Thessaly; and hence, perhaps, the fable of the metamorphosis of Daphne, daughter of that river. It also, with classic propriety, adorns mounts Ida and Athos. There has long been some confusion between the laurel and the bay *; the former,

---

* Gray (the poet) observes and corrects an error on this subject. Speaking of a work he had just been reading, he says, the author "fancies the Roman laurus to be our laurel; though it is undoubtedly the bay-tree, which is *odoratum*, and, I believe, still called Lauro or Alloro at Rome."

though but known to modern times, has been believed by the ignorant to be the tree so venerated by " the mighty dead," the classic bay; the mistake may have originated in the latter being called laurel and its fruit being named bayes. Various writers have, however, come forward to assert its just rights, and restore to it its " local habitation and its name; " and the Laurus nobilis at last occupies that station in botanical works which, from its " old renown," it may fairly demand.

It was commonly believed by the ancients that the bay was instrumental in quickening the fancy, and exciting poetic inspiration; on which account the votaries of the muse were wont to sleep on its leaves.

The bay being held sacred to Apollo, the poet only seems to have a right to claim it as his own; but we have the authority of the ancients for extending the privilege to other aspirants after fame, as in early times it was seen by turns encircling the brows of the prince and warrior, as well as the poet. The Abbé Resnel considers the custom of crowning poets to be coëval with poetry itself; but other writers fix it at a much later date, even so late as the reign of Domitian, before which period, they affirm, no authentic account can be produced of such ceremonial ever being observed. It certainly appears strange that the Greeks — a people so ready to appreciate and reward merit of every·kind and degree — should forget the claims of the poet.

In these rites the bay was generally in requisition, though sometimes it was left to the choice of the individual whether bay, ivy, or myrtle, should compose his crown.

After contemplating its lofty destiny, as being the meed of the conqueror and the poet, there is something inexpressibly ludicrous in viewing the part it was formerly called to sustain in the festivities of Christmas : —

> " Then the grim *boar's head* frown'd on high,
> Crested with *bays* and rosemary."

Alas ! " how fallen from its high estate ! "

Evelyn says that while young this tree grows best under its " mother's shade, where nothing else will thrive ; " thus forming a comment on a passage in Virgil, translated by Martin, " The little Parnassian bay shelters itself under the shade of its mother." It also possesses, in a remarkable degree, the power of resuscitation : long after it has appeared dead, if left undisturbed, it will put forth leaves again, and assume its pristine vigour.· On this account a sprig of bay was formerly thrown on the coffin at the time of interment ;

being considered a striking symbol of the resurrection of the dead.

Many more interesting anecdotes and associations connected with the bay might be added to the above, but we must leave them to other hands, and notice its noble rival, the palm.

———————

THE PALM.

PALMA.

"Meek souls there are, who little deem
   Their daily strife an angel's theme,
   Or that the rod they take so calm
   Shall prove in heaven the martyr's palm."

WHATEVER praise may be awarded to the bay, there are few but will be disposed to give yet higher honour to the palm. Like its classic associate (with which it was often blended), it was considered an appropriate meed for the victor, but more generally it was reserved

for religious triumphs; and from this, as well as from
the prominent place it occupies in Holy Writ, we feel
the epithet of "celestial palm," bestowed on it by Pope,
not inapplicable. But we must leave these considerations for a while, till its natural peculiarities and real
utility have been briefly noticed.

There are many beautiful species of this magnificent
genus; one of the most beautiful of which, perhaps, is
found on the shores of the Orinoco, which,

> ———— " Like a sunborn king,
> Its proud tiara spreads elate,"

far above the dense mass of foliage amongst which it
grows. Its graceful beauty, however, is but a secondary
consideration; for when the country is under water —
a circumstance of frequent occurrence — it affords both
food and habitation to the natives. The whole scene is
thus forcibly described by the poet : —

> " Wide o'er his isles the branching Oronoque
> Rolls a brown deluge; and the native drives
> To dwell aloft on life-sustaining trees,
> At once his dome, his robe, his food, and arms."

Valuable, however, as this species is, it yields in importance to the cocoa-nut, sago, and date palms; more

especially the latter, *par éminence,* the palm of the ancients; the cultivation of which, throughout the East,
is considered a matter of great moment. Indeed, " in
the interior of Barbary, Egypt, Arabia, and the dry districts of Syria, it is almost the sole object of agriculture;
and the date harvest is anticipated with as much anxiety,
and, when a plentiful one, is attended with as general
rejoicing, as the vintage in the South of Europe." And
no wonder; for " this tree alone," as Raleigh says,
" giveth unto man whatsoever his life beggeth at nature's
hand;" forming, either in a fresh or prepared state,
the chief sustenance of the inhabitants during ten
months of the year. Its trunk, also, supplies a sap from
which a fermented liquor is made, called " Lakhlsy."
Thomson thus refers to it : —

> " And from the palm to draw the fresh'ning wine."

And Waller says, —

> " The sweet Palmettos a new Bacchus yield,
>   With leaves as ample as the broadest shield ;
>   Under the shadow of whose friendly boughs,
>   They sit carousing where their liquor flows."

Whilst the method of procuring it, which is by breaking off the crown and hollowing the top of the trunk into the shape of a basin, seems thus alluded to by Milton : —

> " The savoury pulp they chew, and in the rind
> Still as they thirsted ,scoop the brimming stream."

Nor must we forget, while enumerating the benefits it confers, to notice the effect of a palm, or group of palms, when seen in the distance, on the mind of the weary and thirsty wanderer of the desert. Not only is the shelter it offers from a vertical sun anticipated with feelings he only can experience, but he thinks of the fountain which springs at its foot; and, in his eagerness to obtain the life-dispensing draught, he hurries on, forgetful alike of difficulties and fatigue: and seldom or never is he disappointed; for "though it often grows in apparently dry and sterile soil, a subterraneous supply of water may be always calculated upon:" confirmatory of which fact is the assertion of Sir Sidney Smith, who, when in Egypt, informed the British officers that they might always find water by digging to the roots of a palm tree. Other travellers also make the same statement.

The palm is a tree of slow growth; and, "even in the

M

soil and clime most congenial, old trees do not gain
above a foot in height in five years; so that, supposing
the increase uniform, the age of a tree sixty feet high
cannot be less than three hundred years." Though
there are fine forests of the date-palm in the more
luxuriant parts of the province of Valencia, and though
it grows abundantly in some other places in the south
of Europe, yet it diminishes both in size and beauty as
it approaches the temperate zones; and it is only in its
own proper climate, which has a mean annual temperature of from 75° to 83° of Fahrenheit, that it perfects
its fruit. South America, it is said, contains the finest
portion of the palm country; but, from early association,
perhaps, when we name this tree, we generally connect
it with the East, and immediately turn our eyes towards
Egypt, Arabia, and

> " The neighbouring land, whose palmy shore
> The silver Jordan laves."

In the latter country it grew plentifully, especially in
the plain of Jericho, with the distinctive title of which,
" the City of Palms," we are early familiarised.

The graceful form of the palm, its growing on the
verge of great deserts where few other vegetable productions will live, and the high esteem in which it is

held in Eastern countries, on account of its real utility, have secured for it the favour of the muse. Milton names it with other trees as forming " the enclosure green" which encircled the garden of Eden : —

——— " Overhead upgrew
Insuperable height of loftiest shade,
Cedar, and pine, and fir, and branching palm ;
A sylvan scene. "

But we must turn from the page of poetry to that of inspiration, as the palm derives its chief honour from the frequent notice it there obtains. In the book of Ecclesiasticus its stately beauty furnishes Wisdom with an apt similitude : — " I was exalted like a palm tree in Engaddi." " To express or delineate prosperity and opulence," says Bishop Lowth, " a comparison is assumed from the cedar or the palm : " thus, in the ninety-second Psalm, verse 12., — " The righteous shall flourish like the palm tree." Its common use in religious ceremonies has been before adverted to ; indeed, its introduction into all the solemn festivals of the Jews was by divine appointment ; and these were so frequent, that Judea was typified by the palm tree upon the coins of Vespasian and Titus.

Since the Christian era it is associated with more

touching and glorious recollections, — our Saviour's
triumphal entry into Jesusalem; which event was
formerly commemorated in Christian countries by carrying branches of palm in solemn procession: on that
account the Sunday before Easter still retains the name
of Palm Sunday. There is yet another honour reserved
for it. When earthly distinctions have passed away "as
a tale that is told," the palm is held forth in the Book of
Revelations as symbolic of the final victory of the just.

"After this I beheld, and, lo, a great multitude,
which no man could number, of all nations, and kin-
dreds, and people, and tongues, stood before the Lamb,
clothed with white robes, and palms in their hands."

After considering the different species of fame which
these two noble trees memorialize, — the one " of the
earth, earthy," the other, that which shall subsist eter-
nally, — who would hesitate which to prefer?

> " If endless ages can outweigh an hour
> Let not the laurel, but the palm inspire."

Yes; let the bay still crown the warrior and the
poet, — the Christian, humbly, yet hopefully, aspires to
the palm !

TO THE BAY.

Not around the peaceful bower
　　Should thy verdant branches twine,
Though thy leaves through wintry hour
　　With unchanging lustre shine;
There are fitter scenes than this for thy bloom:
　　On the poet's lofty brow
　　Let thy classic garlands glow,
　　Or, if he lieth low,
　　　　On his tomb.

Or, return'd from well-fought field,
　　When the victor throws aside
Both his dinted helm and shield,
　　And his sword in crimson dyed,
O'er his trophies let thy green branches wave;
　　For what so fit a meed
　　From the country he has freed,
　　As the laurel-wreath decreed
　　　　To the brave?

Such the deeds thou lovest to grace —
　　But, thou proud triumphal tree,

Soon shall time thy wreaths deface,
And those deeds forgotten be;
Born of earth, with things of earth they must die:
But there is a fame shall last,
When earth's flitting glory's past,
And a branch no adverse blast
Shall destroy.

'Tis, like thee, the victor's meed;
But it decks not poet's grave,
Nor the warrior's martial deed,
No — 'tis only seen to wave
Where the martyr's honour'd dust doth repose;
Or his, who broke the gloom
Long of pagan lands the doom,
And made " the desert bloom
As the rose." *

* How beauteous are the feet of those who bear
Mercy to man, glad tidings to despair!
Far from the mountain's top they lovelier seem
Than moonlight dews, or morning's rosy beam;
Sweeter the voice than spell or hymning sphere,
And listening angels hush their harps to hear."

But where's the power of thought
   Which may pierce those scenes sublime,
When the Christian's fight is fought,
   And o'er Sin and Death and Time
Through heaven-imparted might, he hath won;
   When he joins the glorious band
   Who as crowned victors stand,
   Each with palm-branch in his hand,
     Round the throne?

THE BANYAN TREE.

FICUS INDICA.

" The fig-tree, not that kind for fruit renown'd,
  But such as at this day to Indians known,
  In Malabar or Deccan spreads her arms,
  Branching so broad and long, that in the ground
  The bended twigs take root, and daughters grow
  About the mother tree, a pillar'd shade
  High overarch'd, and echoing walks between."

So many and so definite are the descriptions, both in prose and verse, of the Banyan, that the mind feels almost familiar with it, though perhaps no tree is more strongly impressed with foreign lineaments. In our conservatories, " foreigners from many lands,"

" Unconscious of a less propitious clime,"

are seen mingling in social union; not only flowers and shrubs, but trees of considerable magnitude. Such, however, is the astonishing bulk of this leafy giant, that the broad bosom of earth, and the overarching

sky, alone afford " ample room and verge enough " for
the full developement of its fair proportions. What a
graphic description we have of its mode of growth and
general appearance, not only in the motto above quoted,
but in the following lines by Southey ! They convey
a stronger and more perfect impression than any sketch
could do : —

" 'Twas a fair scene wherein they stood,
 A green and sunny glade amid the wood,
 And in the midst an aged Banyan grew.
  It was a goodly sight to see
  That venerable tree,
 For o'er the lawn, irregularly spread,
 Fifty straight columns propp'd its lofty head,
  And many a long depending shoot,
  Seeking to strike its root,
 Straight like a plummet, grew toward the ground.
  * * * * * *
 Others of younger growth, unmov'd, were hung
 Like stone drops from the cavern's fretted height.
  Beneath was smooth and fair to sight,
 Nor weeds nor briers deformed the natural floor :
 And through the leafy cope which bower'd it o'er
  Came gleams of chequer'd light.
 So like a temple it did seem, that there
 A pious heart's first impulse would be prayer."

And the voice of prayer *is* heard within this sylvan oratory; but, alas! it is not directed to Him who alone can answer prayer, but "unto gods that cannot save."

"Each tree," says Forbes, "is itself a grove, and some are of an amazing size, as they are continually increasing, and, contrary to most other animal and vegetable productions, seem exempted from decay; for every branch from the main body throws out its roots, at first in small fibres, several yards from the ground, which continually grow thicker, until by a gradual descent they reach its surface, where, striking in, they increase to a large trunk, and become a parent tree, throwing out new branches from the top. These in time suspend their roots, and receiving nourishment from the earth, swell into trunks, and shoot forth other branches: thus continuing in a state of progression so long as the first parent of them all supplies her sustenance, forming the most beautiful walks, vistas, and cool recesses that can be imagined."

Well may the poet speak of

———— " The maze
Embowering endless, of the Indian fig."

The leaves of this tree are large, soft, and of a lively

green; the fruit is a small fig, when ripe of a bright scarlet; affording sustenance to monkeys, squirrels, peacocks, and various birds which dwell among the branches.

The astonishing magnitude of this gigantic tree recalls some sweet lines by Montgomery, occasioned by the subjoined remarks of Dr. Carey, the Baptist missionary at Mysore : — " With great labour I have preserved, for six or seven years, the common field daisy, which came up accidentally in some English earth; but my whole stock now is one plant. The proportion of *small* plants in this country is very inconsiderable, the greater number of our vegetable productions being either large shrubs, immense climbers, or timber trees." The copy of verses alluded to is too long to insert the whole; but one of the stanzas, immediately bearing on the subject, we cannot forbear quoting : —

> " Thrice welcome, little English flower !
>   To this resplendent hemisphere,
>   Where Flora's giant offspring tower
>   In gorgeous liveries all the year ;
>   Thou, only thou, art *little* here,
>   Like worth unfriended and unknown,
>   Yet to my British heart more dear
>   Than all the torrid zone."

In another stanza of the same poem the splendid monotony of India is strikingly contrasted with the freshness and variety which characterise both the climate and productions of England. Instead of periodical returns of dry and wet weather, we have showers and sunshine throughout the year; instead of trees chiefly evergreens, and which, in consequence, even if the climate permitted it, could display but little change of tint, ours are mostly of a description which show the alternations of season. The freshness of spring, the splendour of summer, the gorgeousness of autumn, and the desolation of winter, are all exhibited by our British sylva. When we consider, too, that extremes, either of heat or cold, tend to deteriorate both the mind and the body of the human species; above all, when we reflect that "the glory of the Lord has risen on our land," while "gross darkness covers" those regions, who would not say with the poet, —

> "England, with all thy faults, I love thee still, —
> My country?"

We read of India's " spicèd air,"
  Her forests vast, her gorgeous bowers;
Of trees, which at one moment bear
  The richest fruit, the fairest flowers.
But they for whom these wonders smile,
  Who breathe this " spicèd air," are slaves;
Then hail, to thee, my native isle !
  Whose only vassals are the waves.

We read of trees of mighty size,
  Each forming in "itself a grove;"
Whose drooping boughs, to Fancy's eyes,
  Seem into aisles and cloisters wove.
Pierce we the shade, — what meets the sight?
  Idolatry's polluted shrine.
Then hail, dear England ! land of light !
  Where heaven-revealed truth doth shine.

Give me, fair land, thy healthful gales,
  With sweet but simple perfume fraught;
Give me thy forests, mountains, dales.
  What though they do not cumber thought
With such oppressive grandeur, — still
  They're grand and fair enough for me:

There's health upon thy breezy hill,—
   There's shelter 'neath thy greenwood tree.

The cots, — where dwell thy peasant sons,
   Each with its garden-plot so gay;
The dingle, where the mill-stream runs,
   The green, where children meet to play.
The village church, but barely scann'd,
   Just peeping forth from tufted trees;
Oh ! what in India's gorgeous land
   May be compared with scenes like these?

The spreading Banyan's proud array
   I heed not, while the oak is ours,
Nor would I change thy ivy spray
   For " creepers threading ruby flowers."
But, oh ! though many a precious boon
   To thee, my native land, be given,
A gem yet brighter decks thy crown,—
   Thine is " the light that leads to Heaven ! "

THE CEDAR.

PINUS CEDRUS.

"The cedar proud and tall."

It has been remarked that the fig, the vine, and the olive, are richer in scriptural associations than any other trees: this statement must be recalled, for even they, honoured as they are, yield to the cedar. The cedar of Lebanon! — what a crowd of interesting recollections rush on the mind at the very mention of it; for we meet with it in almost every page of the Bible! In the poetical parts, it is made the constant symbol of prosperity, majesty, and duration.

It is called upon to figure the flourishing state of "the righteous:" —

"He shall grow like a cedar in Lebanon."

To denote the prosperity of the Jewish nation,—

"The boughs thereof were like the goodly cedars."

Nay, even to aid our conceptions of the grandeur and majesty of the Messiah, —

" His countenance is like Lebanon, excellent as the cedars."

Every subject it is employed to illustrate, every epithet by which it is distinguished, speaks its unrivalled pre-eminence. Thus, in the 104th psalm, —

" The *trees of the Lord* are full of sap ; even the cedars of Libanus, which he hath planted."

In another psalm, along with all that is grand and beautiful in nature, it alone is called upon by name, as if to represent " all the stately inhabitants of the forest," to adore the great Creator,

" Praise the Lord, mountains and all hills ; fruitful trees and all cedars."

The accuracy of its description by the sacred writers, even when using it figuratively, is worthy of remark. Its great strength is implied by the very power mentioned as effecting its destruction : " The *voice of the Lord* breaketh the cedars, yea, the Lord breaketh the cedars of Lebanon ; " while its mode of growth and general appearance is as strikingly intimated by Ezekiel, in his highly-wrought comparison of the Assyrian monarch to " a cedar in Lebanon with fair branches, and with a shadowing shroud, and of an high stature, and his top was among the thick boughs. His boughs were multiplied, and his branches became long. The fir trees were not like his boughs, nor the chestnut-trees like his branches, nor any tree in the garden of God like unto him for beauty." " In this description of the prophet," says Gilpin, " the two principal characteristics of the cedar are marked: first, the multiplicity and length of its branches; and, secondly, its close-woven leafy canopy, when, having attained its perfect growth, no distinction of any spiry head or leading branch appears; but, in the language of Eastern sublimity, ' its top is among the thick boughs.' "

But we must reluctantly turn from these notices of sacred literature to those of science, and state, as briefly as the subject will allow, a few other points in its natural history.

Though there are many sylvan aspirants to the title and dignity of the cedar, there are in fact but two species of this genus, — the cedar of Lebanon (Pinus cedrus), and the Indian cedar (Pinus deodara), neither of which are known in the European market as a timber tree. The cedar partakes of the nature and character both of the pine and larch; the leaves are evergreen like those of the former, but smaller, less glossy, and

N

not so blue in colour; whilst they resemble the latter in being bound together in a little tuft, the pines having seldom more than from two to five leaves in each sheath.

No tree exceeds the cedar in durability; ages roll away without apparently making an impression on it. There is something, too, in its wood so offensive to the worm (that destructive little foe to most of the giants of the forest) as entirely to secure it from its depredations: on this account, its timber was chosen by the ancients for the images of their gods, for embalming the bodies of their deceased kings and heroes, and also for the coffins in which they were enclosed. It is of a fine colour and most pleasant scent; but unless great care be observed in the drying of it, it is said to be liable to split.

The cedar was introduced into England about one hundred and fifty years ago; but, though so ornamental and so patient of our climate, it has hitherto been but sparingly cultivated. It likes humidity of soil and atmosphere, a circumstance not overlooked in the sacred writings:—"How goodly are thy tents, O Jacob, and thy tabernacles, O Israel! as the valleys are they spread forth, as *cedar-trees beside the waters.*"

We are, however, so accustomed to connect it with

mountain scenery, from its being so constantly associated with Lebanon, that it is almost difficult to imagine it adorning the plain; but it seems as if it would thrive, with a very little care, in any situation; and perhaps, if the attention of cultivators be properly drawn towards it, we shall see it completely naturalised amongst us, and mingling its patrician dignity with the more sturdy robustness of the oak. From its own peculiar habitat, Mount Lebanon, the cedar has now almost entirely disappeared; a very small number of trees, and some of them decayed and shattered from age, are all that are now left of the boasted forests that formerly crowned that ancient mountain.

As there is but one other true species of this genus (Pinus deodara), we must not pass it altogether without notice; the more so, because it is very closely allied, both in appearance and in general properties, to its more celebrated rival. In durability it is said even to excel it; its timber is exceedingly compact, and abounds in aromatic resin, which fits it for the very great elevation at which it is found to grow; it can, indeed, bear greater variation of temperature than either the spruces or pines, for it is seen both higher and lower on the Himalaya than they. Its numerous beneficial and ornamental qualities give it the same sacred character, in the eyes of the Hindoos, as the cedar of Lebanon has in ours; and consequently we find it blending with their mythology, adorning their temples, and perfuming their sacrifices. A tree of so much beauty, usefulness, and renown as the cedar, must necessarily have acquired much poetic homage. Its height, its durability, its far-spreading shade, its "dainty odours," have each been brought into view.

Homer selects it, on account of the fragrance of its wood, as fuel for the cave of Calypso: —

"Large was the grot, in which the nymph he found
(The fair-hair'd nymph, with every beauty crown'd)
She sat and sung; the rocks resound her lays:
The cave was brighten'd with a rising blaze;
Cedar and frankincense, an od'rous pile,
Flam'd on the hearth, and wide perfum'd the isle."

Its use in building is adverted to by Virgil: —

"Yet Heaven their various plants for use designs;
For houses, cedars; and for shipping, pines."

Milton describes

———— "the garden of God with cedars crown'd,
Above all hills."

In Henry the Sixth, Shakspeare compares the dying
Warwick to a falling cedar : —

" Thus yields the cedar to the axe's edge,
  Whose arms gave shelter to the princely eagle,
  Under whose shade the ramping lion slept;
  Whose top-branch over-peer'd Jove's spreading tree,
  And kept low shrubs from winter's powerful wind."

And in Henry the Eighth, he makes Cranmer say, when
predicting the birth of King James, —

———— " He shall flourish,
And like a mountain cedar reach his branches
To all the plains about him."

Innumerable are the passages, both in ancient and
modern poetry, which have reference to this noble tree;
but one more must suffice, and that from Thomson, who
gives such a magic beauty to every subject he undertakes
to illustrate. We almost feel the balmy gale playing
around us, and see the cedar wave, as we read the following lines : —

" Or thrown at gayer ease, on some fair brow,
  Let me behold, by breezy murmurs cool'd,
  Broad o'er my head the verdant cedar wave,
  And high palmettos lift their graceful shade."

The cedar is said to possess the very peculiar property of "raising its branches to support the load which may oppress them." This property is mentioned by many writers, and, amongst others, it is incidentally alluded to by Sir Walter Scott, as follows: "Brave men as well as cowards are subject to nervous agitation; with this difference, that the one sinks under it, like the vine under the hail-storm, and the other collects his energies to shake it off, as the cedar of Lebanon is said to elevate its boughs to disperse the snow which accumulates upon them."

"Said'st thou the cedar in its mountain-hold
Did meet with drooping boughs the glance of summer,
But that when storms were rife, no longer then
Unstrung and nerveless, with a quick rebound
Recovering all at once its stately beauty,
It rais'd itself to meet the falling snows?"

"I did: but prithee what has that to do
With this calm burial-place, or those low graves,
Apart from all the rest, which thou hast stood

So long contemplating? Methinks the yew
Would blend more naturally with churchyard musings
Than doth the kingly cedar."

       " True, most true:
Yet in that trait of sylvan character
(Which I would deem more than a traveller's tale)
Something there is that minded me (how aptly
Thyself shalt judge when thou hast heard my story)
Of one who occupies the nearest grave.
Wilt hear the tale? Come, sit we on this bank;
The scene above, around us — these green mounds,
Yon sacred pile, the calm which eve now sends
Through earth and sky, will suit my theme, and aid.

 " Didst mark that decent cottage by the green,
Deck'd with such creeping plants as best become
A rustic dwelling, woodbine, and brier-rose,
And that pale clematis we wont to call
The Traveller's Joy? Well — some years since,
A widow dwelt there with her only child.
She came from distant parts, but why she chose
This lonely nook none ever rightly knew;
Certain it is she was not hither drawn
Either by kindred or by social ties;

A stranger came she, and such still remain'd;
For though each kindly act of neighbourhood
She took and gave with seemliest courtesy,
Companionship she sought not: her sweet boy,
And her own thoughts, seem'd all the world to her.
She look'd like one who had seen better days,
Such, too, her manners show'd : her pallid brow
Wore traces more of sorrow than of time,
But what her cause of grief she never told:
This much her garb reveal'd — that she had kept
A widow's vigils, shed a widow's tears.
Seldom she smil'd, save when her blooming boy,
Now her sole earthly prop, some tale would tell
With childhood's sweet, beguiling playfulness,
Or when at his close suit she shar'd some game
Which call'd perforce for two, then would she try
To throw aside her gentle pensiveness,
And give him answering smiles.   As for the child,—
He doated on his mother.   Acts, not words,
Were his o'erflowing heart's interpreters;
When village clocks announced a double boon,
Freedom alike to scholar and to master,
He play'd not with his mates upon the green,
But hasten'd home to trim the garden plot,
And tie such flowers as droop'd from their own weight,

Because he knew his mother's love for flowers.
There was one rose-bush — far or near its like
Could not be found — a sort of village-wonder —
That bush was her delight, and therefore his;
And had it been endow'd with consciousness,
He scarce had tended it with nicer care;
Duly 'twas watch'd and water'd, duly pruned,
And it repaid him with unrivall'd bloom.
Well may you guess how such sweet winning ways
Would steal into her heart, her *widow'd heart;*
And oft, when through the lattice she look'd forth
And saw him busy at his duteous task,
Tears would she shed, but they were not of grief.
But I am tedious, and will hasten on.

" Years pass'd, and told on each. With him you saw
Youth verging on to manhood; but in heart
The same as ever, duteous, tender, kind.
With her, alas! they left far other tokens,
Deep wrinkles, blanched locks, and failing strength:
Such was Time's dealing with the outward frame.
The mind he touch'd more gently; rather say,
He aided sweet religion's proper task,
In healing grief's dark ravages; and now
Life's setting sun had merg'd from that dark cloud

Which veil'd its noontide beam.   Her faith and hope
Had found sure anchorage, and she appear'd
To grow in meetness for a better world.
One tie, with strength almost unlawful, bound
Her soul to earth; she had one idol left:
True it was hidden in her heart of hearts;
But He, whose eye pierces that sanctuary,
Beheld it shrin'd where He alone should be;
Beheld, and frown'd.   He did prepare a worm,
Which smote the gourd she had too fondly priz'd,
And soon it droop'd.   To speak without a figure,
Her son, her *only* son, fell sick and died.
'Twere vain to tell thee how, with almost more
Than mother's love, she nurs'd him in his sickness;
Night saw her at her post, and early dawn;
Nature in her seem'd chang'd, for food, sleep, rest,
Appear'd no longer needful to sustain
Th' animal life.   How long this might have been
'Twere hard to say; but fever did its work
Swiftly and surely; on the fourteenth day
He lay a lifeless corpse, and she became
A childless mother !

                    " Ah ! if words were vain
To picture what she felt when hope's soft beam

Mingled, though tremblingly, with anxious fear,
How doubly vain their power when hope was none!
You might have seen her watching by the dead
As if he were but slumb'ring, and anon
Look at the clock, as if to calculate
How long he yet might sleep; then sudden wake
To the full knowledge of her wretchedness,
Till sorrow darken'd into deep despair.
Thus pass'd those few sad days which intervene
Between the dying and the funeral hour:
And now the bell with intermittent toll
Proclaim'd the last solemnities at hand.
Its awful summons from the hamlets round
Brought many mourners to the widow's cot,
Anxious to show this tribute of respect
Both to the dead and living.   Some there were
Who strove to speak of comfort, but the words
Died on the lip; some wept aloud, — but she,
She — the chief mourner, neither sigh'd nor wept;
Widow'd and childless, hers was that deep woe
Which tears can neither measure nor relieve.

" Slow through the churchyard path, with funeral dirge
The corpse was borne; she followed close behind:
And some among that simple village train

Appear'd expectant that an unseen hand
Again would stay the bier — awake the dead —
And to the widow her lost son restore.
Ah, foolish thought! on, on they slowly moved:
No hand omnipotent outstretch'd to save:
The grave receiv'd its tenant, ' dust to dust '—
Those solemn words — were spoken, and the earth
Shower'd on the coffin, told the rite was o'er.

" There were who would have follow'd to her home
The poor bereaved one, that she might not feel
' So utterly alone;' but there was that
In her deep, voiceless grief, which seem'd to check
Th' expression of the sympathy it rous'd.
So, to her desolate home alone she went,
Enter'd the dreary threshold — clos'd the door.
What met her gaze? the now forsaken couch,
Wearing the impress still — heart-sickening sight! —
Of the lov'd burden it so lately bore.
With shudd'ring dread, she turn'd her eye away,
And in its meaningless survey, it fell,
Shall I say, heav'n-directed, or by chance?
On her son's Bible; with a trembling hand
She open'd it, scarce knowing what she did,
And hurriedly from text to text she glanc'd.

But th' abstracted mind no import gave
To threat'ning, or to promise; both alike
Fell unregarded; till, as with a spell,
These solemn verses fix'd both eye and soul:
' Brethren, I would not have ye ignorant
Concerning them that sleep, that ye weep not
Even as others do which have no hope;
For if we do believe that Jesus died
And rose again, even so them also
Which sleep in Jesus, God will bring with Him.'
She read them o'er and o'er, until it seem'd
To her excited mind as if a voice,
' A still, small voice,' did breathe them in her ear.
She knew that he *so slept*, he — whom she mourn'd,
Then wherefore thus in hopeless sorrow grieve?

" The rock was smitten, — tears, soft, healing tears,
Gush'd from her aged eyes; she knelt, she pray'd, —
Pray'd from her inmost heart; and she did find,
By the sweet hopes which dawn'd upon her heart,
The earnest of an answer ere she rose.
Hard task was hers, and slow was she to learn,
But her resource was prayer; and strength was given
When most 'twas needed, so that she bore up
Against the cruel storm, which all had deem'd

Even to the earth would crush her; and at last
Upon the sod, the very sod that wrapt
Her soul's dear idol, could she kneel and say,
' Thou, Lord, didst give, and Thou didst take away :
For ever blessed be thy holy name !'

" Now know'st thou why that story of the cedar
Blent with my musings by those lowly graves."

THE SANDAL TREE.

SANTALUM.

———— " Groves of myrrh,
And flowering odours, cassia, nard, and balm ·
A wilderness of sweets; for Nature here
Wanton'd as in her prime, and play'd at will,
Her virgin fancies pouring forth more sweet,
Wild above rule or art; enormous bliss ! "

THIS exquisitely glowing picture of the bowers of
Paradise seems, as regards the vegetable productions of
the East, even at the present day, scarcely over-charged.
The very prose descriptions of modern travellers assume
much of the character of poetry from the varied and
fervid terms they are constrained to use in order to convey even a faint idea of the fragrance and beauty of the
oriental forests and groves —

" Groves, whose rich trees weep odorous gums and balm."

Palms of various species, guavas, plaintains, bananas,
tamarinds, mangos, sandal trees, and a long train of
et cæteras, are seen adorning both their woods and

hedgerows, often yielding support to the most lovely climbing plants.

"There sportive creepers, threading ruby flowers
    On emerald stalks, each vernal arch entwin'd,
        Luxuriant though confin'd;
    He heard sweet-breathing gales in whispers tell
    From what young bloom they sipp'd their spicy smell."

The sandal tree grows in many parts of India, and is one of the most valuable productions on the Malabar coast, where, when permitted by the traders, it attains a considerable size, somewhat resembling the myrtle in appearance. Forbes describes it as a beautiful tree, the branches regular and tapering; the leaf, like the narrow willow, shorter and delicately soft, with pendulous bunches of small flowers, sometimes white and sometimes red. It was supposed the white and yellow sandal-wood was the produce of different trees, but Miller denies this. When the Sandal has acquired some bulk, in common with most old Indian trees, it becomes coloured towards the centre, and this heart-timber, as it may be called, is the part most esteemed, not only on account of its tint, but also for its superior fragrance and durability; the exterior part being white and scent-less. This inner wood is much used for cabinets and other ornamental furniture, and forms an article of great importance in oriental commerce.

The Sandal is one of the sacred trees of the Hindoos. It is made frequent mention of by their ancient writers, both in poetry and prose. It is planted near their temples, and from its shavings and dust an aromatic oil is extracted, which, with other odoriferous offerings, is used by them in their sacrifices and religious ceremonies, particularly at the cremation of the bodies of the higher castes. An allusion to their dark idolatry at once casts a veil over —

> " This gay profusion of luxurious bliss,
> This pomp of nature ; "

and thankfully we turn to our own favoured island, externally, indeed, " less winning fair," but blest with the " light that leads to heaven ; " and whilst ours is that inspired volume which directs fallen man to " the Tree whose leaves are for the healing of the nations," — whilst we live under a mild government and equal laws, —

> " Let India boast her plants, nor envy we
> The weeping amber, and the balmy tree,
> While by our oaks the precious loads are borne,
> And realms commanded which those trees adorn."

O

But this should not be our only feeling: the more we appreciate our own advantages, the more desirous should we be to extend them to others; and, both nationally and individually, help on the day, when one song shall employ all people, — " Worthy is the Lamb that was slain ! "

" O shame on thee, thou peerless tree,
　That such debasing task is thine,
To yield thy boasted fragrancy
　As incense on an idol's shrine ! "

Such were my musings as I caught
　The lovely Sandal's perfumed sigh:
Then paused, heart-stricken, for methought
　Elsewhere the censure might apply.

Born in an age, a land, of light,
　'Tis true I yield not worship vain
To sun by day, to moon by night,
　Or golden image on the plain * :

* Daniel, iii.

Yet often at that solemn hour
  When to my closet I repair,
And fain 'gainst all would " shut the door,"
  Save Him, who hears and answers prayer;

Yea, even then, — oh, thought abhorr'd !
  How do I start appall'd to find
That " other gods beside the Lord"
  Within my bosom are enshrined !

Some thought I care not to control,
  Some cherished friend, some darling aim:
These have the homage of my soul,
  E'en whilst I name Jehovah's name.

Then point the well-earn'd censure home
  Erst lavish'd on the sandal tree,
Till never more an idol come,
  False heart ! between thy God and thee.

For thee, fair tree, whose sweets misplaced,
  Have roused this self-condemning strain,
Grateful, I wish thou ne'er may'st waste
  Those sweets on idol-shrine again.

No ! soon may He,—whose word is might,
  Whose will is triumph,—so unveil
His glory in the heathen's sight,
  That shrine and votary both may fail.

May error's darkling shades depart
  Where'er His banners are unfurl'd;
His altar be the human heart,—
  His temple a converted world !

THE ARBUTUS.

ARBUTUS UNEDO.*

——————— " Great Spring, before,
Green'd all the year, and fruits and blossoms blush'd
In social sweetness on the self-same bough."

IF this were the only criterion of the golden age, we might fancy, whilst gazing on the Arbutus, that it was returned again, for this beautiful tree is indeed

——" loaden with fairest fruit,
Blossoms, and fruit at once."

But, alas! short would be the illusion; a momentary glance at some neighbouring tree would at once remind us we are yet in a fading, fallen world: for the Arbutus is profuse of its fruit and flowers when all the rest of the grove have "fallen into the sere, the yellow leaf."

* Arbutus unedo : the meaning for this word, " you will eat but one."

This beautiful peculiarity, however, though it does sometimes feed fanciful conceits and baseless visions, makes the Arbutus a very valuable addition to the lawn and the shrubbery, where it is now no longer the rarity which Evelyn describes it to have been in his day. It is valuable also in such situations on another account; its old leaves never fall off till replaced by new ones, so that it is clothed with verdure all the winter through; its foliage, both in shape and colour, has a resemblance to that of the bay. "It rises," says Miller, "to from twenty to thirty feet in height, but rarely with an upright stem. It usually puts forth branches very near the ground; the berries are roughened with the tubercles of the seeds." The Arbutus is a native of the South of Europe, and many parts of Asia: it is also found wild on the barren limestone rocks near the lake of Killarney, where its fruit is eaten by the natives: this is also the case in Spain and Italy. In very early times we are told this practice was universal; but surely not in the golden age to which we have before alluded, otherwise we should be tempted to believe, that, at least in the article of food, the nineteenth century surpassed "those prime of days."

This tree is not without classical fame. It is mentioned by Virgil, Horace, and Ovid. The former, it is true, does not associate it with any thing very sublime or ennobling, for he chiefly recommends it as peculiarly agreeable to goats in the winter, when other sustenance fails; for basket-work, and for the purposes of engrafting : —

> " Rough arbute slips into a hazel bough
> Are oft engrafted."

Horace, however, gives it higher praise. He commends it for its shade; and Ovid for the beauty of its ruby fruit. It has received but little poetical notice in our own country; less, surely, than it deserves; but its not being much cultivated here till lately may account satisfactorily for the omission, without impugning the taste of such of our forefathers as were skilled " to sing and build the lofty rhyme."

We find it thus noticed in modern poetry : —

> ———— " The leafy Arbute spreads
> A snow of blossoms, and on every bough
> Its vermeil fruitage glitters to the sun."

And again : —

> ———— " Glowing bright
> Beneath the various foliage, widely spreads

The Arbutus, and rears his scarlet fruit
Luxuriant, mantling o'er the craggy steeps."

There are several species of this beautiful genus;
most of which affect mountainous situations. The An-
drachne, or oriental strawberry tree, grows both on
Mounts Ida and Helicon, and the Arbutus alpina is
seen clothing the Lapland Alps, from their summits to
their base; it also cheers the dreary district around the
White Sea, and other inhospitable regions.

Youthful maiden, wouldst thou know
Why, to deck thy sunny brow,
I this graceful garland bring?
Not for lack of brighter thing,
Not because the grove, now sere,
Proffers nothing sweet or fair,
Not because the garden's prime
Vanish'd with the summer-time;

No, — if roses nigh at hand
Woo'd me now with whisper bland,
Or the lily, purest gem,
Sought to form thy diadem,
Still I would this chaplet twine
Round that laughing brow of thine.
Wherefore? Youthful maiden, try
To resolve the mystery.

Mark upon this lovely bough
How in social beauty grow
Flowers and fruit, a fairy throng,
Fitting theme for poet's song;
Sure not brighter wreaths than this
Graced the famed Hesperides.
Yet a lovelier sight I know:
(Ay, thou read'st my riddle now)
'Tis, — when in the social bower
Wisdom's fruit, and youth's fair flower,
(Combination rare as sweet)
On the self-same scion meet.

Youthful maiden, I would see
These rare graces meet in thee;

'Twas this gentle hint to breathe
That for thee I pluck'd this wreath:
Take it, then, and on thy brow
Let its mingled beauty glow,
But the moral it imparts, —
Wear *that* in thy heart of hearts.

SORROWFUL NYCTANTHES.

NYCTANTHES, ARBOR-TRISTIS.

Is not your world a mournful one
  When your sisters close their eyes,
And your soft breath meets not a lingering tone
  Of song in the starry skies?
Take ye no joy in the day-spring's mirth
  When it kindles the sparks of dew?
And the thousand strains of the forest's mirth
  Shall they gladden all but you?

IT is said of the birds which inhabit the torrid zone, that what they gain in beauty of plumage over those of colder climates, they lose in melody; for when, as the poet says, —

——— "Nature bids them shine
Array'd in all the beauteous beams of day,
Yet, frugal still, she humbles them in song."

Not so, however, with the productions of the vegetable world: they, for the most part, possess both a gorgeousness of bloom, and a richness of fragrance, of which, one may readily conceive, such as have not visited those lands can form no idea: —

> " Another Flora there, of bolder hues,
>   And richer sweets, beyond our gardens' pride,
>   Plays o'er the fields, and showers with sudden hand
>   Exuberant spring."

The same also may be said of their sylva. To one whose eye has been accustomed to the plain, unpretending grandeur of our woods, how strange must be the appearance of forest trees, covered with large, showy, odoriferous flowers,

> " Blossoms and fruits at once of golden hue; "

and of creepers, which he only knows as choice hot-house specimens, festooning their stems and branches as in England the ivy does those of the oak and the elm.

All oriental travellers are eloquent in praise of the exquisite perfume and astonishing luxuriance of the gardens, groves, and forests of Hindoostan. Forbes, speaking of the Nabob's gardens on Narranseer Lake, says, " After sunset, the atmosphere was filled with fragrance from the orange trees, champahs, and oriental jasmines, wafted by gentle breezes over the lake." Not less "sweet is the breath of morn:" after describing

the shrubs, trees, and creeping plants that adorn the
enclosed lands in Dhuboy, and which in the rainy season are profusely covered with blossoms of every hue,
he adds, " their *early* fragrance is delicious; the nightly
dews, impregnated by the odours, exhale their short-
lived sweets, and render a morning walk delightful."
This glowing sketch brings to mind a sentiment in a
Turkish ode : —

> " The sweetness of the bower has made the air so fragrant,
> That the dew before it falls is changed into rose-water ; "

which is thus rhythmically rendered by Sir William
Jones : —

> " The dew-drops sprinkled, by the musky gale
> Are changed to essence, ere they reach the dale."

This elegant and profound scholar speaks with the
most delighted enthusiasm of the vegetable wonders of
the East : sometimes appearing almost at a loss for terms
to describe their variety, beauty, and fragrancy ; and to
his spirit of research we are indebted for an introduction
to many exquisite Indian plants before unknown.

Amongst those which he mentions with the most lavish
encomiums, are the Nyctanthes, a tribe nearly allied to
the jasmines ; indeed, it is a disputed point amongst

botanists to which genus some of the different species belong. The proverbially fragrant sambac, or zambac, according to Sir W. Jones, is called Nava mallica, or many-flowered nyctanthes, and Gærtner also considered it of the same genus; whilst Miller classes it with the jasmines. When the learned differ, who may decide? In two delightful qualities, however, the rival genera certainly agree, namely, in their beauty and perfume.

The tree selected for our purpose is the sép'hálicá, after the Sanscrit nomenclature; the *sorrowful* nyctanthes of Linnæus (*triste* being the epithet he always gave to night-blowing flowers). It is thus described by our author: " This *gay* tree (for nothing sorrowful appears in its nature) spreads its rich odour to a considerable distance every evening; but at sunrise it sheds most of its night-flowers, which are collected with care for the use of perfumers and dyers. My pundits unanimously assure me, that the plant before us is the sép'hálicá, thus named because bees are supposed to sleep on its blossoms."

This nocturnal fragrance has a twofold spell; it not only regales the senses, but affects the imagination, by reminding us of that incense of the heart which is offered " in secret to Him who seeth in secret."

Silence and Darkness ! mighty are your spells
To search the spirit ! Guilt, that walks by day
With shameless front, and every fear repels,
Trembles like sentenc'd victim 'neath your sway;
For ye do tear each false disguise away,
And summon forth from memory's dread abyss
Follies and crimes, a long and black array,
Till, all unmask'd, he feels the thing he is, —
One to whom cleaves that curse which shuts the soul
      from bliss !

Not so with him whose heart is purified '
By heavenly grace; he loves your solemn reign;
He joys to see the pomp of day subside,
And trace your distant footsteps on the plain.
By day he communes with his fellow-men,
By night with God ! 'Tis then his spirit pours
Its holiest sacrifice of prayer and praise;
Like that fam'd tree, the pride of eastern bowers,
Which keeps its choicest sweets for midnight's stilly hours.

Men call it sad — that fair and fragrant tree —
Because it wakens while the forest sleeps;
As false they deem of him who silently
Through the still night his prayerful vigil keeps.

Ah! little do they know, even when he weeps,
How much of peace blends with his very tears,
Healing as dew, whose balmy nectar steeps
The sun-smit flower: while Hope, sweet Hope! appears,
An iris on the cloud, and smiles away his fears.

Silence and Darkness! soon the hour will come
When all must brave ye, for that all must die:
The night of death, the silence of the tomb!
These are realities which none may fly.
Thrice happy they who, when that hour is nigh,
Do feel their faith secure, their sins forgiven:
Soon 'twill be past; and then to ear and eye
What sounds, what sights of rapture shall be given!
For darkness, endless day! — for silence, songs of
      Heaven!

THE IVY.

HEDERA HELIX.

"Oh! how could Fancy crown with *thee*,
    In ancient days, the god of wine,
  And bid thee at the banquet be,
    Companion of the vine?
Thy home, wild plant, is where each sound
  Of revelry hath long been o'er,
Where song's full notes once peal'd around,
  But now are heard no more."

WE may indeed wonder, with the writer of these sweet lines, that the ivy should be desecrated to such unhallowed purposes. Besides the consideration of its usual haunts, there is something so sombre in its appearance as makes it seem but little akin to revelry. One might almost imagine that in wreathing the goblet with its graceful branches, garnished with handsome but poisonous berries, it was designed to point a moral by alluding to "the sweet poison of misused wine."

We are indebted to the ivy for the picturesque beauty it throws around every object to which it at-

P

taches itself: no architectural ornament, however classical, no tracery, however light and elegant, can vie in
graceful effect with this " wild tapestry." But not only
is the eye indebted to it; the imagination also shares
in the obligation for the touching imagery it supplies.
Springing wherever there is ruin and decay, it decks
indiscriminately " the loftiest height" and " the humblest
grave;" and with such exquisite grace, that we doubt
whether Adam, to whom his fair consort (according to
the poet) assigned the task of directing " the clasping
ivy where to climb," could have twined it more tastefully.

Besides decorating the ruined remains of feudal
and monastic splendour, there is not a more beautiful
or characteristic feature of forest scenery than this trail-
ing plant. Every where it may be seen, covering the
ground with its natural mosaic, and climbing the tallest
trees, especially such as are dead or dying (for which it
has a decided preference), round which it throws its
verdant garlands, as if to hide the traces of decay.
Once arrived at their summit, where further support is
denied, it is necessitated to assume more independence
of character, and it then makes an effort to sustain itself;
to effect which its slight flexible stems become short
and woody. In this position, its leaf also undergoes a

change: from being lobed, it becomes heart-shaped; then too it puts forth its umbels of pretty pale green flowers, which first show themselves in October, and continue, in mild seasons, through December, and are then succeeded by large black berries, which are fully formed in February, but do not ripen till April.

The eulogisers of the ivy, however, must not forget that it has had its calumniators, by whom it has been sometimes considered a fit emblem of perfidy and ingratitude. Shakspeare insinuates this, when, in " The Tempest," he makes Prospero say of his treacherous brother,—

   ———— " He was
  The ivy which had hid my princely trunk,
  And suck'd my verdure out on't."

And in another play he entitles it " usurping ivy." Nor has it met with more mercy from some modern authors, one of whom thus pointedly condemns it : —

  " The oak that rears it from the ground,
   And bears its tendrils to the skies,
  Feels at its heart the rankling wound,
   And in its poisonous arms he dies."

To these charges we offer the following eloquent extract from the author of " Les Etudes de la Nature,"

who regards the ivy as the symbol of unchanging friendship : — " Rien (dit-il) ne peut le séparer de l'arbre
qu'il embrasse une fois, il le pare de son feuillage dans
la saison cruelle où ses branches noircies ne soutiennent
plus que des frimas ; compagnon de ses destinées, il tombe
quand on le renverse ; la mort même ne l'en détache
pas, et il décore de sa constante verdure le tronc tout
desséché de l'appui qu'il adopta."

Hast thou e'er seen the moon's soft splendour
   Sleep peaceful on some ruin'd pile,
Gilding with radiance mild and tender
   Each broken arch and mouldering aisle ?

Hast thou e'er seen the ivy clinging
   Round fragments broken and decay'd,
As if its mantling wreaths 't were flinging
   To hide the breaches Time had made ?

Oh ! thus, should care or sorrow wound thee,
   Be Friendship's soft endearment thine,
And fondest sympathy around thee
   As close her thousand tendrils twine.

And when, at last, each youthful token
   Shall yield to wasting and decay,
And thou like arch or column broken,
   Shalt feel proud manhood's strength give way;

Oh ! then may Love, by time unshaken,
   Around its earliest prop still cling,
(For when was mouldering arch forsaken
   By the fond wreath it caused to spring?)

Still may one smile, as moonbeam tender,
   E'en to the last unwearied shine,
Gilding thy manhood's waning splendour,
   And oh, may that one smile be mine !

THE ASO'CA.

—————— " But come, my muse,
Thou, like the harmless bee, shalt freely range
From mead to mead bright with exalted flowers,
Through palmy shades and aromatic woods."

THE Asóca is another oriental beauty on which Sir
William Jones bestows the warmest praise. He describes it as a new genus; and as he only gives the
vernacular name, not the Linnæan, it would be difficult
to discover further particulars of its history than those
with which he himself has favoured us. He strongly
objects to the genuine names of Asiatic plants being
superseded by trivial, and, according to his opinion,
unmeaning appellations. The former are mostly very
comprehensive, and highly poetical; thus the Hindoos
give the scarlet hibiscus a title which answers to " gem
of the sun;" the ipomea they call Cámalatá, or " Love's
creeper" (after the Indian Cupid) ; and to all beautiful
aquatic flowers they give the general name of " Cu-
muda," which signifies " delight of the waters."

But to return to the Asóca, the description of which
is as follows: — " Flowers fascicled, fragrant just after

sunset and before sunrise, when they are fresh with morning and evening dew; beautifully diversified with tints of orange-scarlet, of pale yellow, and of bright orange, which grows deeper every day, and forms a variety of shades according to the age of each blossom that opens in the fascicle. The vegetable world scarcely exhibits a richer sight than an Asóca tree in full bloom. It is about as high as an ordinary cherry-tree."

The peculiarity mentioned by this elegant scholar of the late and early fragrance of the Asóca is of a kind that addresses itself at once to the imagination. The whole volume of nature (secondary only to that of revelation) is indeed replete with pure and holy lessons; and if duly and properly studied, would not only enrich the mind and elevate the fancy, but amend the heart.

Pilgrim of life! if friends caress,
   If youth's gay flowers thy path be strewing,
If joy so ready is to bless
   He yields his gifts without the wooing;

Oh! pray that He whose hand has spread
 Thy path of bliss may guide thee ever,
Pour His own dews upon thy head,
 And in "all time of wealth deliver;"
And like that tree which hastes to shower
 Its fragrance soon as morn has given
Her liquid balm, oh! ever pour
 The incense of thy soul to heaven!

Pilgrim of life! if grief's dim eve,
 Or deeper night be fallen upon thee,
If youth be past — if friends deceive —
 Friends, who once fondly wooed and won thee;
Oh! hie thee, mourner, to the bower
 What time dim eve is duly flinging
Her chilly dews on tree and flower,
 And mark the sweetness thence up-springing
Meekly to bow the willing head,
 E'en when the heart is blighted — riven;
To trust, to praise, when light is fled, —
 This — this is incense meet for heaven!

THE MISLETOE.

VISCUM ALBA.

"Not far away, for ages past had stood
An old, inviolated, sacred wood;
Whose gloomy boughs, thick interwoven, made
A chilly, cheerless, everlasting shade:
There barbarous priests some dreadful power adore,
And lustrate every tree with human gore;
The pious worshippers approach not near,
But shun their gods, and kneel with distant fear."

FROM time immemorial, trees, either standing apart in solitary majesty, or congregated in groves and forests, have been consecrated to the solemnities of religion. " Paradise itself," says Evelyn, "was but a kind of nemorous temple, planted by God himself, and given to man." This appropriation of them to sacred purposes may be traced even in the patriarchal ages. Abraham, we are told, " planted a grove in Beer-sheba, and called there on the name of the everlasting God." It was in a bush, or, as some commentators render it, a grove, that the angel of the Lord appeared to Moses " in the

wilderness of Mount Sinai:" and when the same glorious Being visited Gideon, "he came and sat under
an oak."

Trees have also been solemnized by funeral obsequies.
When "Deborah, Rebekah's nurse, died, she was buried
beneath Bethel, under an oak; and the name of it was
called Allon-bachuth, which signifies oak of weeping."
The bones of Saul and his sons had also a similar place
of sepulchre.

Such was the sanctity of trees and groves in the
earlier ages of the world; and such it continues still in
many places. Nor can we wonder at it, for their
shadowy recesses seem made for meditation : —

> " Still let me pierce into the midnight depth
> Of yonder grove, of wildest, largest growth :
> These are the haunts of meditation,—these
> The scenes where ancient bards the inspiring breath
> Ecstatic felt; and, from this world retir'd,
> Convers'd with angels and immortal forms,
> On gracious errands bent."

These "angel visits," always "few and far between," have long ceased to bless our world; but he
who has a mind attuned to devotion may, in these
" sweet retired solitudes," enjoy yet higher and holier

communion; he may, like our first parents — but with what different feelings! — hear " the voice of the Lord God walking in the garden in the cool of the day."

This is the true and proper use of these natural oratories. But, alas! they were soon desecrated to other purposes. Even the Israelites themselves soon borrowed the customs of their heathen neighbours, and devoted those very groves to idol-worship which their fathers had planted and consecrated to the one true God. " They set up images and groves," says the sacred text, " in every high hill, and under every green tree; and there they burnt incense in all high places, as did the heathen whom the Lord carried away before them." And again : — " They sacrifice upon the tops of the mountains, and burn incense upon the hills, under oaks, and poplars, and elms, because the shadow thereof is good." Hence the needful prohibition, " Thou shalt not plant a grove of any trees near unto the altar of the Lord thy God."

Thus if we cast our eye through the deeps of time, travelling from the East to the West, we shall find all nations, — the Israelites, the Persians, the Egyptians, the Grecians, the Romans, — each had their sacred groves, over which certain deities presided, whence oracles spake, and where priests and priestesses officiated, till

at last we arrive in Britain, and find the Druid per-
forming his horrid rites under our native oak.

Could we give credence to the poet, we should recall
the harsh epithet we have bestowed on the superstitious
observances of Druidism.   He, more lenient, says, —

> " There, where the spreading consecrated boughs
> Fed the sage misletoe, the *holy* Druids
> Lay wrapt in moral musings."

Truth, however, which is often called in to correct the
dreams of fiction, speaks another language, and gives
a widely different character of their religion; for though
it is true they held some few primary truths in greater
purity and distinctness than could be found in the mythology even of Greece or Rome, yet these were blended
with a mass of error, and were made to sanction the
most bloody and abominable superstitions.

We have been led very naturally to this train of
thought by the subject selected for illustration, — the
far-famed misletoe.   The utmost solemnity was used in
the gathering of it; it took place always at the close of
the year, when the moon was just six days old.   Two
white bulls, which had never felt the yoke, were fastened
by their horns to the fortunate oak whereon the misletoe

had been discovered; a priest, clad in a white vesture, then ascended the tree, and detached the plant with a golden hook or bill, whilst others stood ready to receive it in a white woollen cloth: this done, they then prepared to offer the best of their flocks and herds in sacrifice, " mumbling many orisons, and praying devoutly that it would please God to bless this gift of his to the good and benefit of all those to whom he had vouchsafed to give it." Water, in which it had been steeped, they considered a panacea for diseases of every description; hence the name they gave it, " omnia sanans, or all-heal."

Having no attachment to earth, it was considered of celestial origin; it was held in the greatest veneration by the Druids, and indeed by most of the northern nations.

Many are the fables attached to this really singular plant: and it must be owned that its peculiar habits, the obscure mode of its propagation, &c. might almost countenance the superstitious regard in which it was held in those dark ages when ignorance and credulity reigned paramount over the human mind. The horrors with which it was associated in the bloody and cruel rites of Druidism, have probably obtained for it, in the following quotation from Shakspeare, " a local habitation and a name" by no means enviable : —

> " A barren and detested vale you see it is:
> The trees, though summer, yet forlorn and lean :
> O'ercome with moss and baleful mistletoe ;
> Here never shines the sun, here nothing breeds
> Unless the nightly owl, or fatal raven."

Connected as it is with gloomy reminiscences, it is somewhat strange that this plant should ever administer to " heart-easing mirth;" and yet, wherever old customs are preserved,

> " Forth to the woods do the merry men go
> To gather in the mistleto ; "

and it is chosen, as it were, to preside over the Christmas gambols; at least in the servants' hall or the kitchen, where a large bunch is hung up in great state, and is the occasion of much merriment.

The misletoe belongs to a genus containing twelve species, one only of which, viscum alba, is found in our groves. It is mostly seen on the apple-tree, the haw-thorn, and the lime; Sir J. E. Smith adds the oak, though most other botanists affirm it is but very rarely found on that tree. This species is also a native of many parts of Europe and Japan.

The manner of its propagation is thus described by Miller : — ". The misletoe thrush, which feeds upon the berries of this plant in winter when it is ripe, doth open the seed from tree to tree; for the viscous part of the berry which immediately surrounds the seed, doth sometimes fasten it to the outward part of the bird's beak, which to get disengaged of, he strikes his beak at the branches of a neighbouring tree, and so leaves the seed sticking by this viscous matter to the bark, which, if it lights upon a smooth part of the tree, will fasten itself, and the following winter put out leaves, and grow."

Its parasitical character has suggested the following stanzas.

" A parasite ! I would not be,
　　For worlds, that servile thing ;
　Not royalty itself, from me
　E'er homage won of heart or knee ;
　　To Power I would not cling
　(Like this vile plant to oaken bough),
　Though it had kingdoms to bestow !"

'T is proudly said — yet pause — for Power
 A crown not always wears;
Oft hundred-headed (as of yore
The monster, famed in classic lore,)
 Its Proteus-form appears:
And thus disguised from mortal ken
Hast thou ne'er worshipp'd in its train?

Not always with aspiring aim
 The plant thou dost despise,
Seeks out the forest-king, — 't will claim
From trees of meaner growth and name
 The wish'd-for help to rise:
Thus, he who boasts he ne'er has bow'd
To kings — oft basely courts the crowd.

Then when thou seest the misletoe
 Hang with its bunches green,
On hawthorn or on wilding's bough,
Ere thou condemn'st it pause lest thou
 Hast like delinquent been.
Far off are courts, and crowns, and kings,
But men may rise by meaner things.

Believe me, Freedom ne'er did mate
  With dark ambition's crew;
She shuns " the rebel's noisy hate,"
Not less than " tyrant's sceptred state;"
  Yet honour yields where due.
Submiss not servile, — firm not proud, —
She worships neither king nor crowd.

THE GUELDER-ROSE, or WAY-FARING TREE.

VIBURNUM LANTANA.

" Way-faring tree! what ancient claim
　　Hast thou to that right pleasant name?
　　Was it that some faint pilgrim came
　　　　Unhopedly to thee,
　　In the brown desert's weary way
　　'Mid toil and thirst's consuming sway,
　　And there as 'neath thy shade he lay,
　　　　Bless'd the way-faring tree?
　　Or is it that thou lov'st to show
　　Thy coronals of fragrant snow
　　Like life's spontaneous joys that flow
　　　　In paths by thousands beat?
　　Whate'er it be, I love it well;
　　A name, methinks, that surely fell
　　From poet, in some evening dell
　　　　Wandering with fancies sweet."

THE way-faring tree is a native of most countries of
Europe, those only excepted which are situated far to
the north. It is found chiefly on a limestone soil in
woods and hedges, but is said to delight most of all in

the vicinity of roads. It puts forth its many-flowered cymes, in scent resembling the hawthorn, towards the middle of May, and perfects its berries in autumn, which in an immature state are red on the outside and yellow on the other, but which when fully ripe are quite black.

This tree belongs to a genus containing many species, of which the favourite little winter-flowering shrub laurustinus is one, and the well-known elder another. A very elegant variety may be met with in almost every ornamental plantation. Who is not familiar with the garden guelder-rose, or snowball, which when in bloom harmonises so well with all the gayer shrubs of spring? How beautifully descriptive of its general appearance and mode of growth are these lines by Cowper, where, however, he groups it with more sombre associates; for he speaks of it, as

> " Throwing up into the darkest gloom
> Of neighbouring cypress, or more sable yew,
> Its silver globes, light as the foamy surf,
> That the wind severs from the broken waves."

It has also been sketched by the elegant pen of Miss Landon : —

> " Here the guelder rose shall fling
> Silver treasures to the spring "

But to return to our homely subject.

The way-faring tree is partly indebted to its name for popularity; not but that its pretty fragrant flower, might justly entitle it to regard; but many a flowering shrub as pretty and as fragrant we pass without notice, whilst this always obtains a share of observation.

Who gave it this appellation, and wherefore, is left to poetical conjecture; but whatever may have suggested the trivial names of this, and other plants, we are indebted to them for many a pleasant and it may be improving reflection. They supply a text on which the mind delights to make its own comments; and there is scarcely an affection or feeling of which the heart is conscious, that may not be in some degree called into exercise by an acquaintance with the habits, properties, and names of the various productions of the vegetable kingdom.

Hail! sportive Fancy, visionary Power,
Oh! soothly tell me in what favour'd hour
    Thou first didst visit earth?
Didst thou descend upon the earliest ray
Whose magic chased chaotic gloom away,
    And smiled on Nature's birth?

Say, wert thou cradled in the first fair rose
That did in Paradise its sweets disclose,
And with superior loveliness arose
    To reign the queen of flow'rs?
And wert thou rock'd by each soft gale, whose wing
Caught the rich scent that new-born rose did fling
    O'er Eden's blissful bowers?

Or didst thou spring in after years
  From that fair bow which spanned the skies,
  When Phœbus, pitying Nature's tears,
  First gemm'd the falling drops with dyes
So bright, so fair, that of her grief beguiled
She gazed upon the vision — gazed and smiled.

Whate'er thy origin may be,
Sweet Fancy, thou art dear to me;
And whether in the sunny glade
I stray, or pierce the forest-shade;
Whether I tread the moorlands wide,
Or track the brooklet's silver tide,
Or " sometimes wander not unseen
By hedgerow elms, or hillocks green;"
Still be thou nigh, companion dear,
Breathing thy lessons in my ear,

Until I feel, and hear, and see
Sweet, visionary Power, like thee.
For thou canst suit thy varying lore
To sheltered cot, or lonely shore,
To river broad, or tiny rill,
To cultured vale, or barren hill.
There's not a flower can ope its eye
To greet us as we wander by,
Or dewdrop gem the bloomy spray,
Or Zephyr with that dewdrop play,
But, if thy magic thou dispense,
'T is gifted with intelligence.
Sometimes — by virtue of a name
Thou givest to lifeless things a claim
On man's regard; — from its fair bower
How sweetly pleads yon little flower, ·
" Forget me not;" — while further on
The Speedwell breathes its benison.
And here's a fair and fragrant tree,
Which from its name might seem to be
The wanderer's friend; — and so it proves;
For when with weary step he roves,
It greets him on his toilsome way
With flowers which yield the breath of May,

And proffers all it hath of shade
When noon's fierce heats his frame invade.
And while reclined its boughs beneath,
If, Fancy, thou thy spirit breathe
Into each fair and fragrant wreath,
Oh ! then, what thrilling memories,
What thoughts within his bosom rise
Of some fond friend, perchance, who showers
His daily path with fairest flowers,
Who greets him with a smile so sweet,
'T was worth the absence thus to meet.

Or, if a graver mood be thine,
Thou mind'st him of a hand divine;
A friend, all other friends above,
" Whose nature and whose name is love;"
Who marks his steps, appoints his way,
Attempers joy's too fervid ray,
And for the dark and stormy hour
Reserveth still some precious flower;
And Who, when life's rough ways are past,
Receives him to Himself at last.

THE BIRD-CHERRY.

PRUNUS PADUS.

" The cherry here hung for the birds of heaven
Its fruit on high."

THIS beautiful tree, which is now so commonly introduced into our parks and pleasure-grounds, is no
naturalised foreigner, but a real genuine native; for it is
found in situations which cultivation never reached —
situations so wild and inaccessible, as to establish its
aboriginal character to the satisfaction of the most scep-
tical naturalist. In such places, its loose bunches of
snowy flowers, and its light foliage, come out with the
best possible effect, contrasted with the dark hue of the
pines, the stunted oaks, and other rugged features peculiar to mountain scenery. But such, indeed, is its
native gracefulness, that it is a beautiful appendage to
any scene; and

" ————— whether fringing the fell
Or cheering the forest, or gracing the dell,
Or skirting the mountain,
Or shading the fountain,"

it always captivates the fancy, and we are apt to imagine, for the time being, that *that* is the one spot which it was made to adorn. Nor is it only when in flower that it claims our admiration. Its fruit, which ripens towards the end of summer, scarcely yields in beauty to its blossoms; it hangs in long bunches, varying in colour as the season advances, from green to full black. In this state it is a most tempting morsel for the birds: hence its English appellation.

The bird-cherry is indigenous in most parts of Europe; it even opens its fragile flowers to the nipping air of Russia and Siberia. It abounds in the northern counties of England, and is profusely scattered among the woods, and on the borders of the mountain torrents of Scotland. In these natural fastnesses, where it is more likely to escape the stroke of the axe, it often rises to the height of fifteen feet from a stem eighteen inches in diameter, and spreads its branches to a considerable distance.

The wood of the whole genus is very compact, and in some species of a fine colour. In others, especially some of the bird-cherries, it is beautifully marked, which makes it in request for ornamental cabinet work.

When in bloom, no tree, either in the plantation or the forest, bears about it more unequivocally the impress of spring. " To a fanciful view," it might seem that sweet season embodied; and the sight of it must have a tendency to awaken feelings of a hopeful and pleasurable nature. In the hey-day of youth, and health, and joy, the mind, as if by way of contrast to its general tone, is too apt to luxuriate in a sort of morbid melancholy, and "in these sullen fits" it seeks such scenes and associations as are most likely to promote it. A fading flower, a falling leaf, the sober sadness of an autumnal day, have then a charm far beyond the brightest and gayest trophies of spring. Not so in after-life: by that time the heart has generally become so well acquainted with real sorrow, that it has no room for such as is fictitious; and it rather turns from those objects which suggest images of gloom and decay, to such as resuscitate hope and gladness.

Such were the feelings awakened in the mind of the author, when she received the spray of bird-cherry (whence the drawing is taken) from a kind contributor of botanical specimens for this work.

Time was, when shadowy eve
   Was dearer to my heart than smiling morn,
And than the lovely garlands Spring doth weave,
   The faded hues by pensive Autumn worn.

'Twas in my youthful prime,
   When life itself put on the look of Spring;
Ere Care, that ever tracks the steps of Time,
   Seem'd other than a visionary thing.

Untouch'd by real grief,
   E'en from its own excess of joy, my heart
In fancied ills would ofttimes seek relief,
   And sport with Sorrow's yet unvenom'd dart:

But now, when every sigh
   Is fraught, alas! with meaning full and deep;
When Hope resigns her seat to Memory,
   And leaves me o'er her vanish'd dreams to weep;

Oh! now I turn away
   From Autumn's sered wreaths to Spring's gay bloom;
Those all too sadly mind me of decay,
   These bid sweet Hope once more her sway resume.

More chaste, indeed, her glow
 Than erst it was in Youth's enchanting prime;
Then were her dreams of earth alone — but now
 She aids my spirit's flight o'er things of time.

THE CYPRESS.

CUPRESSUS SEMPERVIRENS.

" Dark tree ! still sad when other's grief is fled,
The only constant mourner o'er the dead."

" In nature there is nothing melancholy," says Coleridge, — an assertion which none can gainsay; yet it is an assertion we should have expected from the philosopher rather than the poet; for he whose magic spell invests inanimate objects with life and consciousness, might surely endow them with feelings either " grave or gay, lively or severe," according as his own mind might dictate. If in nature there is nothing actually melancholy, there are both sounds and sights which appear so, and *that*, even independently of association, though doubtless this faculty greatly aids the impression. How different, for instance, the plaintive coo of the dove to the sprightly trill of the lark; the faded foliage of November to the vivid burst of vegetation in May : and if the mind be so disengaged as to be open to impressions from outward things, how different the emotions produced by each! Who can view with similar sensations the birch and the yew, or the hawthorn and the cypress? Does not the one awaken feelings of cheerfulness, the other of gloom?

The cypress is a dark, pyramidal evergreen, growing to a considerable size in a soil and climate favourable to its development. Its proper birthplace is the Levant, particularly the island of Candia, where it grew in such profusion, that the Romans, and after them the Venetians, obtained a considerable revenue from its timber. Though our easterly winds are very prejudicial to it, the cypress does not fear cold in the land of its nativity, for it is seen climbing the snowy top of Mount Ida. From Candia it was brought first to Italy, where it is now so completely naturalised, and forms so prominent and acknowledged a feature in the sylva of that classic country, that no Italian scene is perfect without it.

Bearing in mind the associations connected with this tree, what touching effect, what mournful grace, does it throw over the architectural remains of ancient Rome!

> ———— "come and see
> The cypress, hear the owl, and plod your way
> O'er steps of broken thrones and temples."

" Cypress and ivy, weed and wall-flower grown
　Matted and mass'd together, hillocks heap'd
　On what were chambers, arch-crushed, column strown
　In fragments, choked-up vaults and frescos steep'd
　In subterranean damps, where the owl peep'd,
　Deeming it midnight."

This is desolation! To such mournful relics it is the fittest ornament; yet we sometimes meet with it in livelier company and in gayer scenes, and there too it looks beautiful. "Only figure to yourself," says Gray, writing from Genoa, "a vast semicircular basin, full of fine blue sea, and vessels of all sorts and sizes, some sailing out, some coming in, and others at anchor; and all round it palaces and churches peeping over one another's heads, gardens and marble terraces full of orange and cypress trees, fountains and trellis-works covered with vines, which altogether compose the grandest of theatres." Again he introduces it in a picture, which, though it wants the rhythm, has all the glow of poetry : — "There is a moon! there are stars for you! Do not you hear the fountain? do not you smell the orange flowers? That building you see yonder is the convent of St. Isidore; and that eminence, with the cypress trees and pines upon it, the top of Mount Quirinal."

Such a description costs the mind but little effort to

identify itself with a scene so vividly sketched. We do see the moon and the stars; we do hear the fountain, and mark the cypresses

" Cleave with their dark green cones the silent sky."

The wood of this classical tree is sonorous, fragrant, and of the most imperishable nature; in the latter respect surpassing that of the cedar itself.* It shared, with the cedar, the honour of inclosing the bodies of the illustrious dead, when Egypt and Athens were in their glory, in both which countries it was applied to such purposes.

Hunter enumerates only four species of this genus; later writers extend the number to two and twenty. Rapid as is " the march of mind" in our days, this difference in so few years is surprising, and excites a conjecture how many more may be discovered before science really comes to a stand.

The *true* cypress, as every one knows, is a tree of much classical celebrity. Its name, according to ancient fable,

* It is on record that the doors of St. Peter's, in Rome, were made of cypress wood, and were found perfectly sound after the lapse of eleven hundred years, when, at the command of Eusebius the Fourth, they were superseded by gates of bronze.

was derived from Cyparissa, a youth beloved by Apollo, who, having accidentally killed a favourite stag belonging to his patron, was so concerned at the luckless deed, that he earnestly prayed to share the fate of the beautiful animal he had slain.

It has always been considered the type of grief, and is generally accompanied by some mournful appellative.

Virgil speaks of

" ———— fun'ral cypress rising like a shroud "

Notwithstanding its gloomy character, however, Homer plants it near the cave of Calypso, on account of its fragrance : —

" Poplars and alders ever quivering play'd,
And nodding cypress form'd a fragrant shade."

Why the shafts of Cupid should have been made of this tree, as some writers report, it is difficult to determine; it might be, because then, as now,

" ———— the course of true love never did run smooth."

Its being consecrated to Pluto and Proserpine in those days of dark superstition, causes no surprise: perhaps

our Shakspeare thought of this, when he makes the Earl
of Suffolk, whilst invoking curses on his enemies, wish

" Their sweetest shade a grove of cypress trees."

Consistently with their notions of its character, the
ancient Romans, on the death of any high-born individual, were wont to place a branch of cypress before
the door of the house where the corpse lay previous to
interment; boughs were also strewn on the bier and
borne by the mourners to the grave. These usages are
not altogether obsolete even in our day, for in many
Eastern countries may yet be seen

" The mournful cypress rising round
Tapering from the burial ground."

The Turks, especially, plant this tree with other aro-
matics in their cemeteries, not only from respect to the
dead, but to benefit the living, as the balsamic odour is
supposed to purify the air. Hasselquist speaks of seeing
cypresses of remarkable size and beauty adorning their
burial grounds. It is said the ancients chose this tree
when they celebrated their funeral obsequies, from a
notion that if once cut down it never sprung again.

Viewed in this light, as it has been well observed, " the cypress is no meet emblem for the Christian's grave:" no — " the Gospel, which has brought life and immortality to light," teaches us, that

> " It is not all of life to live,
> Nor all of death to die ; "

" for the trumpet shall sound, and the dead shall be raised."

If it be sleep that seals his brows,
   And softly shuts his eye,
Then whither is the tint of rose
Which childhood's cheek in slumber knows?
   Oh ! where the quick, short sigh,
And gently heaving breast, which tell
To watchful mother all is well?

Too deep such calm for that sweet rest,
 Which he was wont to know,
When on thy fond maternal breast
His cheek and brow were closely prest,
 Not motionless as now,
But varying with each winged dream
That on his infant mind did beam.

Now must his cradle be the tomb,
 His pillow earth supply;
Yet weep not, for since such our doom,
Seems it not sweet in life's first bloom
 To bow the head and die,
Ere scarce the hidden worm hath power
To mar one folding of the flower?

Each year we heave a deeper sigh,
 Our hopes are more o'ercast;
And had *this shaft* flown harmless by,
Think'st thou, that calm as infancy,
 Youth, manhood, age had pass'd?
Or soft had been as thy fond breast
The pillow of his future rest?

Ah! no,—the blow thy hopes which cross'd,
   To him was sent in love;
For whilst to thee a child is lost,
Another seraph swells the host
   Of glorified above;
Then calmly dust to dust resign,
Since gone the gem 'twas wont to shrine.

And let us strew his cradle bed
   With fragrant flowers and fair;
Flowers that beseem the early dead,
Such as do soonest bloom and fade—
   The firstlings of the year;
And when we lay him in his grave,
Let the sad cypress o'er him wave.

The cypress?—nay, that were to throw
   On faith and hope a stain,
By Christian grave ne'er should it grow,
For is't not said, if once laid low
   It never springs again?
Whilst, to thy babe, the dying strife
But usher'd in undying life.

Hear'st thou a new, sweet voice essay
   The strains which angels sing?
See'st thou along the star-paved way
A seraph blest in bright array
   Soar on exultant wing,
With harp in hand, and palm-crown'd brow?
Fond mother, such thine infant now.

And would'st thou round the free — the blest —
   Earth's fetters re-entwine?
Or once again with thorns invest
Those brows, where now sweet peace doth rest,
   And cloudless bliss doth shine?
No — thy sole wish is now, to rise,
And join thy loved one in the skies.

THE HAWTHORN, or MAY.

CRATÆGUS OXYCANTHA.

" Amongst the many buds proclaiming May,
　Decking the fields in holiday's array
　(Striving who shall surpasse in braverie)
　Marke the faire blooming of the hawthorne tree ;
　Who finely cloathed in a robe of white,
　Feeds full the wanton eye with May's delight."

Soon as " the hawthorn whitens," we know that spring
is in its zenith, and looking around we realize the vivid
picture of the poet, —

" And see the country far diffused around,
　One boundless blush, one white-empurpled shower
　Of mingled blossoms."

Various species of hawthorn are common in different
lands; but our own may surely vie with any in beauty
and fragrance. It is amongst the early-leafing trees,
and none put forth a sunnier, richer tint: and then its
blossoms — they are every thing one would wish; their
perfume and appearance are alike exquisite, and fully

entitle it to the post of honour assigned to it by the poet, of being "the virgin flag of Spring." It has also another charm: concealed in its flowery recesses, the little birds "warble their native woodnotes wild," and seem as if they would repay it for their winter's sustenance by the sweetness and variety of their strains. Burns, the poet of nature, makes frequent allusion to this circumstance; thus, in "The Petition of Bruar Water:" —

> " And for the little songster's nest
> The close embowering thorn."

In another poem he again introduces it: —

> " Within yon milk-white hawthorn bush,
> Amang her nestlings sits the thrush;
> Her faithfu' mate will share her toil,
> Or wi' his song her cares beguile."

Yet one more quotation on the same subject, and from the same pen: —

> " The scented birk and hawthorn white
> Across the pool their arms unite,
> Alike to screen the birdie's nest."

Gilpin always speaks disparagingly of this tree; which, in a lover of the picturesque, is matter of wonder;

for the sight of it in full bloom always suggests pastoral or rural images. In describing such images it is never forgotten by the poet. Milton says, —

> " And every shepherd tells his tale,
> Under the hawthorn in the dale."

And Shakspeare, in " Henry the Sixth:"—

> " Gives not a hawthorn bush a sweeter shade
> To shepherds looking on their silly sheep,
> Than doth a rich embroider'd canopy
> To kings that fear their subjects' treachery?
> O! yes, it doth; a thousand fold it doth."

In " The Deserted Village," Goldsmith rather varies the picture, and shows us

> " The hawthorn bush, with seats beneath the shade,
> For talking age and whispering lovers made."

The hawthorn is the usual accompaniment of that characteristic feature of English rural scenery, the village-green. With what truth and beauty has the poet, just quoted, described the merry gambols of which this tree is, we were going to say, the almost sympathising witness, so well does its cheerful, rustic aspect, suit the scene : —

> " How often have I bless'd the coming day
>   When toil remitting lent its turn to play,
>   And all the village train, from labour free,
>   Led up their sports beneath the spreading tree !
>   While many a pastime circled in the shade,
>   The young contending as the old survey'd ;
>   And many a gambol frolick'd o'er the ground,
>   And sleights of art, and feats of strength went round."

Formerly, on May-day and at Whitsuntide, as well as at Christmas, houses, and even churches, were profusely decorated with flowers or evergreens peculiar to the season. This custom is still preserved at Christmas, when almost every temple and every window boasts its sprig of holly: and in some places May-day is thus appropriately ushered in; the hawthorn blossom, when the season is a forward one, being substituted for the evergreen ! These practices, however, — to the joy of some, and to the grief of others, — are now certainly on the decline; but we are assured by the greatest poet of the day, that the feeling which suggested them is still alive. In his beautiful address to May he says, —

> " And if, on this thy natal morn,
>   The pole, from which thy name
>   Hath not departed, stands forlorn
>   Of song, and dance, and game ;

Still from the village-green a vow
Aspires to thee addrest,
Wherever peace is on the brow,
Or love within the breast."

May we be allowed another quotation from the same
author, addressed to the same auspicious season; it will
serve, perhaps, as a useful hint to those who complain
that May is not the beautiful month it used to be : —

" Season of fancy and of hope,
Permit not for one hour
A blossom from thy crown to drop,
Nor add to it a flower !
Keep lovely May as if by touch
Of self-restraining art,
This modest charm of not too much,
Part seen, imagined part."

" They tell me storms o'er life do lower,
They tell me man to grief is born ;
But I have ranged through mead and bower,
Still asking, as I cull'd the flower,
Where lurks the thorn ? "

Avowal sweet of youth's blithe day!
  Made only ere the heart is torn;
Ah! who in after years can say,
With smile incredulously gay,
  Where lurks the thorn?

How true a type this hawthorn bough
  Of youthful dreams in life's first morn;
So thick the fragrant blossoms grow,
What curious eye detects below
  The frequent thorn?

But wait a few brief days, and soon
  That bough, of all its glory shorn,
Its fragrance spent, its blossoms gone,
Will to thine eye show one by one
  Each pointed thorn.

Thus crown'd with light, and link'd with flowers,
  Seems life, in youth's enchanting morn;
But soon, how soon, the tempest lowers,
And, stripping Fancy's fairy bowers,
  Lays bare the thorn!

THE COMMON MAPLE.

ACER CAMPESTRE.

" No tree in all the grove but has its charms,
Though each its hue peculiar ·
Some glossy-leav'd and shining in the sun,
The maple, and the beech of oily nuts
Prolific."

THE common maple belongs to a genus containing
many species, of which it seems to be the only undis-
puted native. It rarely grows to any size, being held
in very little esteem, so little, that Gilpin remarks,
" We seldom see it employed in any nobler service than
in filling up its part in a hedge, in company with thorns
and briars and other ditch trumpery."

But, though disregarded by the moderns, it can draw
upon the past for fame; few trees having been in
greater repute amongst the ancients. It is mentioned
by many of the classical writers. Virgil represents
Æneas at the court of Evander as seated on a maple
throne :—

" On sods of turf he set the soldiers round :
A maple throne raised higher from the ground
Received the Trojan chief."

Doubtless that author selected it on account of the estimation in which it was held for ornamental works.

" In the most high and palmy state of Rome," at least as refers to luxury and refinement, tables, and various other elegant articles, were made out of the knots or swellings of the wood, which, being often beautifully and curiously marked, commanded immense prices.

The enormous sums expended in that madly luxurious age on these fancies, it is supposed, originated the well-known proverb of " *turning the tables* " upon any one : for when the men at any time reproached their wives for their wanton expensiveness in pearls and other rich trifles, they were wont to retort, and *turn the tables* upon their husbands.

Such is the by-gone fame of the maple; and, when we consider that its timber possesses the same beautiful veins and marks now as formerly, it is surprising it should not be in greater demand.

A modern association connected with this tree, but of a totally different character from those already noticed, attaches great interest to it.

Beneath a large maple in Boldre churchyard, in accordance with his own request, lie the remains of the Rev. William Gilpin, whose elegant and interesting work on " Forest Scenery " is familiar to most readers;

and to which the author of this volume is indebted for much valuable information, which she takes this opportunity of gratefully acknowledging.

The sycamore, or great maple, is one of the most noted species of this genus. If not indigenous, against which there seems a well-grounded suspicion, it is at least so far naturalised as to be admitted into Sir J. E. Smith's *English Flora;* where it is spoken of as " common, but not truly wild;" a testimony corroborated by that of Gerarde and Parkinson, who mention it as a stranger in England, and " only planted in walkes and places of pleasure for the shadowe's sake." But, whether a native or a foreigner, it is a noble tree, and the richness and variety of its tints, both in spring and autumn, add so greatly to the beauty of the grove, that none can

> —— " unnoticed pass
> The sycamore, capricious in attire,
> Now green, now tawny, and, ere autumn yet
> Have chang'd the woods, in scarlet honours bright."

On incision, the sycamore yields a liquid containing saccharine matter. This property is, indeed, common to other species of the maple family, one of which derives its distinctive title, Acer saccharinum, from the abundant supply of sugar contained in the sap.

Before earthenware was so much in use as it now is, the wood both of the greater and lesser maple was in considerable demand for various household utensils. We are familiar, with it in poetry, as furnishing those bowls and dishes which are as needful appendages to a hermit's cell, as a mirror to a lady's toilet: this seems implied in the following quotations: —

> " His dwelling, a recess in some rude rock,
> Books, beads, and maple-dish his meagre stock."

> ———— " Many a visitant
> Had sat within his hospitable cave ;
> From his maple-bowl the unpolluted spring
> Drunk fearless, and with him partook the bread
> That his pale lips most reverently had bless'd."

> ———— " No tradition tells
> That ever hermit dipp'd his maple-dish
> In the sweet spring that lurks mid yon green fields."

> " For who would rob a hermit of his weeds,
> His few books, or his beads, or maple-dish ? "

Some give to the sycamore alone the special honour of thus ministering to the frugal comfort of these mistaken recluses; but, as it was of comparatively late introduction, and as our own native maple was certainly used for domestic purposes, why may it not share this "help to fame?"

"And may at last my weary age
Find out some peaceful hermitage,
The hairy gown, the mossy cell,
Where I may sit and rightly spell
Of every star that heaven doth shew,
And every herb that sips the dew,
Till old experience doth attain
To something of prophetic strain."

O Poesy, bewitching power!
What fascinations are thy dower!
Thou dwellest in a fairy round,
Thou treadest on enchanted ground;
"The common air, the sun, the skies,
To thee are opening paradise."
Thy touch can turn to more than gold
The meanest object we behold;
Thy master spell all nature owns,
Thou giv'st a meaning to the tones

Of summer breeze and wintry gale;
Thou add'st a shade to midnight's veil,
Splendour to noon, —to pensive eve
More touching softness, — and dost weave
For morn a coronal of flowers,
Such as but grow in Fancy's bowers.
While Science, with unpitying hand,
" Unweaves the rainbow," thou dost stand
In tranced gaze, but dost not pause,
Pleased with th' effect, to ask the cause.

Ev'n now, what charms thy magic spell
Has thrown around a hermit's cell :
Who that has read that witching lay,
" But long'd for wings to flee away"
To some sweet spot of rest, and share
The hermit's cell, the hermit's fare,
Such fare, as Nature in the wild
Can proffer to her lowly child,
Served up in quaint but fitting sort,
In dish of veined maple wrought;
And there to learn the saintly lore
Which holy Nature has in store
For those who view with thoughtful eye
The wonders of the earth and sky,

And, freed from turmoil and annoy,
There woo sweet Peace, and Peace enjoy.

Peace ! — fond enthusiast, — deem'st thou, then,
She needs must live in lonely glen,
In desert wilds, or mountain cave,
Lull'd by the fountain's welling wave,
Or by the many-voiced trees,
Slow, waving in the midnight breeze?

Ah ! foolish one — recall that thought;
There 's not on earth one certain spot
Where Peace doth make her home.   Oh ! yes,
One home she hath, one dwelling-place,
From which, for heav'n she scarce would part —
The loving, lowly, contrite heart !
She hath (though rarely there, I ween)
In courts and stately halls been seen ;
More frequent in the humble cot,
Smoothing the peasant's rugged lot ;
In busy mart, and dusky street
Sometimes her gentle form we meet;
And sometimes by the loathsome bed
Where squalid sickness rests her head.

Go, — pierce yon murky alley, where
None ever breathed untainted air,
Where all in vain the glorious sun
Struggles to chase the smoke-wreaths dun:·
Ascend yon broken, winding stair,
Enter that room, what meets thee there?
Nay, shrink not with fastidious pride,
But take thy stand that couch beside;
There, though disease, and want, and pain,
Their victim bind with triple chain,
There shalt thou see earth's noblest sight,
A spirit wing'd for heavenward flight.
There Peace, sweet Peace, has found her way,
And turn'd thick midnight into day.

Now, hie thee hence, and dream no more
Of hermit's cell, and frugal store;
Of skull, of maple-dish, or glass
Which marks how swift the hours do pass;
But ply in Duty's path thy feet,
'T is likeliest there sweet Peace thou'lt meet;
And, if a lowly heart be thine,
Be sure she'll make that heart her shrine.

CHRIST'S THORN.

RHAMNUS PALIURUS.

"'Twas sin marr'd all; and the revolt of man,
That source of evils not exhausted yet.
Garden of God, how terrible the change
Thy groves and lawns then witness'd!"

WHEN Nature "lectures man in heavenly truth," how wise, how various are her lessons! If the mind needs soothing and encouraging, she leads us to those objects which afford pure proofs of the wisdom and goodness of the great Creator; if elevating, she bids us look on "the heavens, the work of His fingers;" if warning, she tells us of the earthquake and the tempest, or, perhaps, with more of pathos, she points to the thorns and the thistles, which beset our every-day path, thence taking occasion to remind us, for whose offence "the prickly curse" was inflicted. "Cursed is the ground for thy sake; thorns also and thistles shall it bring forth to thee." Such was a part of the doom denounced against man when he eat of the forbidden tree.

" Earth felt the wound, and Nature from her seat
 Sighing through all her works, gave sign of woe
 That all was lost. "

The thorn is repeatedly alluded to in Scripture in
the way of threatening. " Thorns and snares are in the
way of the froward." " They have sown wheat, but
they shall reap thorns." " And now go to, I will tell
you what I will do to my vineyard: I will lay it waste;
it shall not be pruned or digged; but there shall come
up briers and thorns." " Thorns shall come up in
her palaces, nettles and brambles in the fortresses
thereof."

These are a few of the many texts where the thorn is
employed, sometimes literally, sometimes figuratively,
to express the sterility and desolation which should visit
those nations and people "whose ways had been perverse
before God."

The species of thorn here signified has furnished a
subject of much ingenious disquisition amongst the
learned. Haselquist fully believes the thorny whin,
(Anonis spinosa) with which, he says, whole fields in
Syria are covered, is the one alluded to in the Scriptures.
It would be difficult, one thinks, to decide on a matter
so entirely conjectural; nor is it a thing of much con-

sequence: thorns and thistles abound every where; and, as " all have sinned," it is more natural to imagine the allusion was not to the peculiar growth of any one climate or country in particular, but to the noxious and troublesome weeds which, without unceasing labour and care, would mock the hopes of the husbandman.

In those climates, however, where various causes conspire most fully to develope vegetative life, thorny shrubs and trees are most abundant, and are armed with stronger and sharper spines than those with which we are familiar. Of such the poet speaks when describing " the wonders of the torrid zone."

> " Here lofty trees, to ancient song unknown,
> The noble sons of potent heat, and floods
> Prone rushing from the clouds, rear high to heaven
> Their thorny stems, and broad around them throw
> Meridian gloom."

Denon says that " nine tenths of the trees and shrubs which compose the thickets in Egypt are armed with inexorable thorns, and allow only an unquiet enjoyment of the shade that is so desirable, from the precaution necessary to guard against them."

Many of the Mimosa genus are signalised by their tremendous spines. Dr. Drummond mentions one, a native of the south of Africa, which from top to bottom is clothed with enormous double thorns, from four to six inches in length, pointing in every direction, and forming thickets impenetrable to every animal except the rhinoceros. The prickly-pear is another formidable plant, which "renders travelling extremely difficult along some parts of the banks of the Missouri, where its spines are so strong, that they will pierce a double shoe sole made of dressed deer skin."

These instances have been selected as bearing the broader lineaments of the curse; and, surely, it would be impossible for a believer in Revelation to traverse the regions where such trees are indigenous, without frequent recurrences to the awful truth with which they appear to stand connected.

Christ's thorn (Rhamnus paliurus) forms a species of a very comprehensive genus. It is described as a tree rising to the height of eight or ten feet, "sending out weak slender branches, garnished with oval leaves of a pale green; the flowers coming out at the wings of the stalk in clusters, almost the length of the young branches; of a greenish-yellow colour. They are succeeded by broad, buckler-shaped seed-vessels, which have borders like the brims of a hat; hence called by the French, porte-chapeau. It is a native of the south

of Europe, Caucasus, and Barbary, and is one of the
most common shrubs in Judæa. This circumstance,
and the pliability of its branches, may account for the
notion that of it the crown of thorns was composed:
hence its name. Haselquist, however, contends for another plant, and states his reasons for the supposition
with some show of probability.

But, after all, these learned disquisitions on such
deeply affecting subjects have more the appearance of
solemn trifling than of any useful tendency.

The thorn is certainly more immediately connected
with gloomy remembrances (gloomy, but salutary); yet
we need not confine our view to such. Though it naturally leads us back to the Fall, it may also remind us
of those happier times, when " there shall be no more
curse," " when the wilderness and the solitary place
shall be glad, and the desert shall rejoice and blossom
as the rose; when, instead of the thorn, shall come up
the fir tree, and instead of the briar, shall come up the
myrtle tree. For the earth shall be full of the knowledge of the Lord, as the waters cover the sea."

Go, child of dust, and from thy brows,
Oh! tear the myrtle and the rose:
If crown thou wear'st, this prickly stem
For thee were fitter diadem,
Since earth thorns bore not, till thy fall
Threw blight and ruin over all.

Gaze on the sky — there was a time
When storms ne'er dimm'd its arch sublime;
Look on the ground — once not a weed
Was mingled with the precious seed;
Behold the rose — the garden's gem,
Once thornless was its graceful stem.

Sad types! yet would that they were all
Which mark'd the sin original!
Ah! go, where lingers pale decay,
And watch life's pulses ebb away;
Go to the grave; — that narrow bed
Must pillow soon thy lonely head.

Ay, weep, for tears become thee well;
Weep whilst thou hear'st yon passing bell, —
So sternly eloquent, — declare
Of what sad doom thou art the heir.

Yes, thou must sicken, thou must die,
The hour is fix'd — it may be nigh.

Yet weep not in despair: ah ! see,
A victim bleeds, He bleeds for thee;
The thorns thy sin had sown He wears;
The death thou earn'dst, for thee He bears;
Then rises from the grave, that thou
Might'st find in death a baffled foe.

Still weep'st thou? ay, but hope and love
Thy spirit's depths now gently move;
Contrition meek — not guilty fears,
Has op'd a fount of holier tears :
Such tears bespeak a soul forgiven,
Such tears awaken joy in heaven.

And does no change, no second birth,
Await the desolated earth ?
Yes, earth, — sore smitten for man's sake,
Shall of his glorious change partake.
Arise, O Lord ! disperse the gloom,
Redeemer, let thy kingdom come !

THE EVERGREEN THORN.

MESPILUS PYRACANTHA.

" Phillyria, here, and pyracantha spread
Their verdant foliage, and berries red
In glowing clusters."

THIS well-known shrub is a native of the South of Europe: it also grows plentifully on Mount Caucasus, in the Chersonesus, and in China. It was introduced here early in the seventeenth century, but has never yet got beyond the pale of the garden or shrubbery, notwithstanding Evelyn's hint that it might be cultivated, with little trouble, for fences and other common purposes. " The pyracantha, paliurus, and like preciouser sorts of thorns and robust evergreens, adorned with caralin berries," says he, " might easily be propagated by seeds, layers, or cuttings, into plenty sufficient to store even these vulgar uses, were men industrious; and then how beautiful and sweet our fields would be ! For there are none of the spinous shrubs more hardy, none that make a more glorious show, none fitter for our defence." But, surely, it would be a sight scarcely less strange than

unwelcome to see our native hawthorn and holly sup-
planted even by this pretty foreigner, which we have
hitherto only been accustomed to observe trained against
houses or walls as an ornamental covering.

The pyracantha puts forth its bunches of delicate
white flowers in May, and may claim · admiration even
then, when the garden is in its glory; but it is when the
fascinations of spring, and summer, and autumn are over
that it is most attractive. Greeting us, when there is little
else to cheer, with its verdant foliage and beautiful scarlet clusters, it reminds us of some friend, who, though
always kind and ready to serve us, reserves his tenderest
and warmest affection for the hour of adversity. In
common with all other trees whose fruit ripens in the
winter, it affords the birds a most timely supply of sustenance, and thus, —

> " For every song that made their summer merry,
> The shrubs repay in winter with a berry."

The beauty of its aspect in that dreary season, and the
associations to which it gives rise, are alluded to in the
following lines, which were presented to a beloved friend
on her birthday in December.

Thou wast not born when merry May
" Hangs out the virgin flag of spring,"
When birds from every bush and spray
    Are caroling.

Thou wast not born when summer throws
Her glory over sky and earth,
Nor did the beam which wakes the rose
    Smile on thy birth.

No; like this shrub which cheers the bower,
What time the threatening storm is rife,
A blessing for the wintry hour
    Thou sprang to life.

And such art still — no summer friend,
Breathing smooth things in Pleasure's ear;
But, oh ! let grief the spirit rend,
    And thou art near.

Then takes thy voice its softest tone,
Then is thy hand upraised to bless,
And then the tender warmth is known
    Of thy caress.

Let others, then, invoke the spring,
And joy to see her buds unclose,
Or from each bush bright summer fling
    Her own sweet rose.

I will not grieve to see them go,
While winter such a wreath can twine;
Ah! see how brightly through the snow
    These berries shine!

What could I less, than love the hour
Which stills the bird, and strips the lea,
Since, oh! to cheer the *social bower*,
    It gave us thee!

THE BOX AND THE LAUREL.

BUXUS.　　PRUNUS.

" When rosemary and bays, the poet's crown,
　Are bawl'd in frequent cries throughout the town,
　Then judge the festival of Christmas near,
　Christmas, the joyous period of the year:
　Now with bright holly all the temples strew,
　With laurel green, and sacred mistletoe."

THE fast fading away of many ancient and pleasant usages, such as ushering in May-day and Christmas, each with its appropriate garland, together with many other unequivocal proofs, remind us that we live in an unimaginative age; an age in which the progress of science, the ingenuity of invention, and the extension and acquirements of commerce, are every where conspicuous; these, in the very nature of things, must soon totally extinguish, not only those few remains of what may be termed *practical* poetry that are as yet spared to us, but even the *spirit* of poetry itself.

The touching practice of strewing the dead, and

crowning the bride with flowers, is now all but obsolete;
and though May is bright and lovely as ever, her accustomed wreath is wanting, as the poet most feelingly reminds us : —

> " Time was, blest Power ! when youths and maids
>   At peep of dawn would rise,
> And wander forth, in forest glades
>   Thy birth to solemnize.
>
> " Though mute the song — to grace the rite
>   Untouch'd the hawthorn bough,
> Thy spirit triumphs o'er the slight :
>   Man changes, but not Thou ! "

Christmas, it is true, is still greeted with verdant trophies; and in many places both houses and churches
are decked with holly, box, &c. This custom is said to
be of questionable origin, and is thus accounted for : —
When idolatry prevailed in our island, the great annual
feast of Saturn was held in December under an oak; at
which ceremony the priests required the worshippers to
bring various evergreens to decorate the naked branches
of their sylvan temple : and, as the first Christian
churches were constructed of boughs, the converts, bor-
rowing the idea from their heathen neighbours, adorned
their rude and leafless edifices at Christmas in like
manner.

T

But the custom itself is harmless, whatever the origin may be; and those persons who have any regard for the manners and observances of other days, will view with regret one usage after another swept away, as if one more link were broken in the chain which connected them with the past, and all its interesting associations.

Various are the evergreens used at the commemoration of the festival of Christmas, but as most of them have already passed under review, the box and the laurel only shall be singled out as representatives of the different claimants for this honour.

The box, of which there is but one species, but many varieties, is a well-known evergeen, growing in every plantation; but, though this is the situation in which we are most accustomed to see it, and that, too, in a dwarfed or clipped condition, it is really an indigenous tree, and, in calcareous soil and dry situations, will rise to the height of ten or twelve feet, with a stem of proportionable thickness. It grows pretty freely on the chalk hills near Dunstable, and on Box Hill in Surrey, to which place, as well as Boxley in Kent, and Boxwell in Gloucestershire, it has given name.

Of all British trees, the box grows the most slowly, which accounts for the heavy, hard, and compact nature of the wood; qualities that make it very valuable for all those works in the construction of which the utmost nicety and precision are required, such as mathematical and musical instruments.

This tree is mentioned by various clasical writers. In reference to its constant verdure, Homer exclaims, —

" Thy groves of box, Cytorus ! ever green."

Its applicability to many useful purposes appears to have been well-known to the ancients. Virgil alludes to its fitness for the turner's trade; and Ovid, to its being employed for flutes or pipes. He says, " Neither does the melody of the voice, nor the long pipe of many-holed box delight them;" while Martial avers, that

———— " Box-combs bear no small part
Of the militia of the female art."

This tree is very common in the various countries of the South, of Europe, and also in Asia, especially in the neighbourhood of Mount Caucasus. The unchanging verdure of its foliage, and the durability of its wood, have always made it an auspicious symbol. As such, Pope introduces it very beautifully in his poem of the Messiah : —

" On rifted rocks, the dragon's late abodes,
   The green reed trembles and the bulrush nods;
   Waste sandy valleys, once perplex'd with thorn,
   The spiry fir and shapely box adorn."

For this use of it he has the best authority. In reference to the Messiah's blessed reign, it is written in the page of inspiration, " I will plant in the wilderness the cedar, the shittah tree, and the myrtle, and the oil tree. I will set in the desert the fir tree, and the pine, and the *box tree* together."

We come next to the laurel (Prunus laurocerasus). It is a native of the Levant, of the Crimea, of Caucasus, and the mountains of Persia. Its introduction here cannot be precisely ascertained; but it was some time before the year 1629, as Parkinson mentions having had a cutting presented to him by Master James Cole, from " a fair tree," cultivated in his own garden with much care, and defended from the winter's severity by throwing a blanket over the top of it. Now, however, it is so entirely naturalised, that it bears all the changes of our climate without injury, produces its beautiful spikes of white sweet-scented flowers in April or May, and its large black berries in September or October; they are seldom, indeed, fully ripe till the latter month. In general, it has more the character of a shrub than a tree;

but it sometimes grows to a considerable size, as, for instance, at Stanmore, near Brighton, the seat of the Earl of Chichester, where there is a hedge of laurel about 220 feet in length, and the trees which compose it have grown to the height of thirty feet. Linnæus makes the laurel one of a very comprehensive genus, classing under the title Prunus the various kinds of plums, cherries, and apricots; whilst Miller separates them into four divisions. Cheering our winter months with its lively and rather warm green leaves (a pleasant contrast to the bluish tint common to most evergreens), it is entitled to our gratitude, and it certainly is greeted with far more favour than is awarded to more beautiful plants which leaf and blossom only in the summer.

'T is Christmas! holy season, hail!
What though the sun is dim and pale,
What though through leafless trees the gale
           Makes sullen moan,
And not a flower is left to tell
           Of summer gone?

Yet, for the memories thou dost bring
The blessed hopes thou bid'st upspring,
I'll greet with gladlier welcoming
           Thy gloomy hours,
Than those bright months which round them fling
           Sunshine and flowers.

Nor wakest thou solemn thoughts alone,
Thy spell the social virtues own:
Who has not felt how sweet the tone,
           The smile how bland,
When thou dost knit again in one
           The household band?

Now stir the fire, and let its glow
Shame the inhospitable snow ;
With all that nature yet can show
    From winter's wreck,
Laurel, and box; and holly bough,
    The casement deck.

'T is joy to hear the sullen north
Summon the rushing tempest forth,
For then around the social hearth
    Friend meeteth friend,
And kindly words and looks of mirth
    Sweet influence lend.

But is't in mirth they always meet ?
Alas ! sometimes a vacant seat
Bespeaks the circle incomplete ;
    Some voice is mute,
Whose welcome was aforetime sweet
    As evening lute.

Then, then indeed a tear will stray,
As they the lessened group survey,
That group with other smiles once gay:
                    And who would blame
The tear affection well may pay
                    To memory's claim?

But whilst from Friendship's silken string
Each year some pearl is scattering,
We 're taught by each lost gem to cling
                    More firm and true
To those yet spared by Time's rude wing, —
                    The cherish'd few.

The cherish'd few! ah! who may tell
What pathos in those words doth dwell:
A voice of meeting and farewell
                    Blends in the sound,
Weaving a monitory spell
                    The heart around.

But hush, my harp, — such plaintive lay
Unseemly greets this blessed day.
How often, when I would be gay,

Thought backward steers
Her course, then joy to grief gives way,

And hopes to fears.

Yet, whilst I muse on change and death,
Till earth seems cleft my feet beneath,
Oh ! may this storm-surviving wreath

A thought supply,
That they who live the life of faith *

" Shall never die !"

* John, xi. 26.

POSTSCRIPT.

IT is with a feeling bordering on regret that the author finds herself at the close of her pleasant task; in the composition of which, and in making the drawings which illustrate it, many an hour has been most agreeably beguiled. Highly gratified would she be if her readers could make the same avowal in reference to the perusal, and encourage her by the assurance that they have accompanied her in her sylvan wanderings with unwearied steps.

Yet, " in the spirit of meekness," she would confess, that to amuse has not been her sole, or even her chief, aim. Throughout the work, she has endeavoured to bear in mind herself, and to impress on others, that " a Christian should be a Christian in the field as well as in the temple;" and that Nature should ever be the handmaid of Devotion: when she is made to take a higher position, she occupies His place, who made the " heavens and the earth, and all the host of them."

In pursuance of her prevailing intention, she would leave one parting caution with her readers, borrowed from that delightful author, whose name has so often appeared in the foregoing pages. Evelyn, after describing with more than his wonted enthusiasm the sylvan beauties of some particular scene, breaks out into the following exhortation, which at once reminds us of what we have lost, and to what we may aspire : —

" But, after all, let us not dwell here too long, whilst the inferences to be derived from those tempting and temporary objects prompt us to raise our contemplations a little on objects yet more worthy our noblest speculations, and all our pains and curiosity, representing that happy state above; namely, a celestial paradise. Let us, I say, suspend our admiration awhile of those terrestrial gaieties, which åre of so short continuance, and raise our thoughts from being too deeply immersed and rooted in them, aspiring after those supernal, more lasting, and glorious abodes; namely, a paradise, not like this of ours, with so much pains and curiosity, made with hands, but eternal in the heavens; where all the trees are trees of life, the flowers all amaranths, all the plants perennial; where those who desire knowledge may fully satiate themselves; taste freely of the fruits of that tree, which cost the first gardener and posterity so dear: no forbidden fruit; no serpent to deceive; none to be deceived ! "

THE END.